Praise for other books by M

FreeBSD Mastery: Storage Essentials

"If you're a FreeBSD (or Linux, or Unix) sysadmin, then you need this book; it has a *lot* of hard-won knowledge, and will save your butt more than you'll be comfortable admitting. If you've read anything else by Lucas, you also know we need him writing more books. Do the right thing and buy this now." – *Slashdot*

"There's plenty of coverage of GEOM, GELI, GDBE, and the other technologies specific to FreeBSD. I for one did not know how GEOM worked, with its consumer/producer model – and I imagine it's complex to dive into when you've got a broken machine next to you. If you are administering FreeBSD systems, especially ones that deal with dedicated storage, you will find this useful." — *DragonFlyBSD Digest*

Sudo Mastery

"It's awesome, it's Lucas, it's sudo. Buy it now." – *Slashdot*

"Michael W Lucas has always been one of my favorite authors because he brings exceptional narrative to information that has the potential to be rather boring. *Sudo Mastery* is no exception." – Chris Sanders, author of Practical Packet Analysis

Absolute OpenBSD, 2nd Edition

"Michael Lucas has done it again." – *cryptednets.org*

"After 13 years of using OpenBSD, I learned something new and useful!" – *Peter Hessler, OpenBSD Journal*

"This is truly an excellent book. It's full of essential material on OpenBSD presented with a sense of humor and an obvious deep knowledge of how this OS works. If you're coming to this book from a Unix background of any kind, you're going to find what you need to quickly become fluent in OpenBSD – both how it works and how to manage it with expertise. I doubt that a better book on OpenBSD could be written." — *Sandra Henry-Stocker, ITWorld.com*

"Do you need this book? If you use OpenBSD, and have not yet achieved guru status, yes, this book is just for you. Even gurus will find valuable things in this book that they did not know... But beyond the OpenBSD aspect, there are great sections on cross-platform applications like *sudo* that are almost enough on their own to justify getting this book. And there are several of those chapters. So: even if you don't use OpenBSD directly, would you like a quick reference on *sudo*, IPv6 networking, and NFS setup? Oh, and also *tftpd*, PXE, and diskless BSD systems? But wait, what if I told you these references came with a free book on OpenBSD installation and configuration?" – *Warren Block, wonkity.com*

"It quickly becomes clear that Michael actually uses OpenBSD and is not a hired gun with a set word count to satisfy... In short, this is not a drive-by book and you will not find any hand waving." – *Michael Dexter, callfortesting.org*

DNSSEC Mastery

"When Michael descends on a topic and produces a book, you can expect the result to contain loads of useful information, presented along with humor and real-life anecdotes so you will want to explore the topic in depth on your own systems." — *Peter Hansteen, author of The Book of PF*

"Pick up this book if you want an easy way to dive into DNSSEC." — *psybermonkey.net*

SSH Mastery

"…one of those technical books that you wouldn't keep on your bookshelf. It's one of the books that will have its bindings bent, and many pages bookmarked sitting near the keyboard." — *Steven K Hicks, SKH:TEC*

"…SSH Mastery is a title that Unix users and system administrators like myself will want to keep within reach…" — *Peter Hansteen, author of The Book of PF*

"This stripping-down of the usual tech-book explanations gives it the immediacy of extended documentation on the Internet. Not the multipage how-to articles used as vehicles for advertising, but an in-depth presentation from someone who used OpenSSH to do a number of things, and paid attention while doing it." — *DragonFlyBSD Digest*

Network Flow Analysis

"Combining a great writing style with lots of technical info, this book provides a learning experience that's both fun and interesting. Not too many technical books can claim that." — *;login: Magazine, October 2010*

"This book is worth its weight in gold, especially if you have to deal with a shoddy ISP who always blames things on your network." — *Utahcon.com*

"The book is a comparatively quick read and will come in handy when troubleshooting and analyzing network problems." —*Dr. Dobbs*

"Network Flow Analysis is a pick for any library strong in network administration and data management. It's the first to show system administrators how to assess, analyze and debut a network using flow analysis, and comes from one of the best technical writers in the networking and security environments." — *Midwest Book Review*

Absolute FreeBSD, 2nd Edition

"I am happy to say that Michael Lucas is probably the best system administration author I've read. I am amazed that he can communicate top-notch content with a sense of humor, while not offending the reader or sounding stupid. When was the last time you could physically feel yourself getting smarter while reading a book? If you are a beginning to average FreeBSD user, Absolute FreeBSD 2nd Ed (AF2E) will deliver that sensation in spades. Even more advanced users will find plenty to enjoy." — *Richard Bejtlich, CSO, MANDIANT, and TaoSecurity blogger*

"Master practitioner Lucas organizes features and functions to make sense in the development environment, and so provides aid and comfort to new users, novices, and those with significant experience alike." — *SciTech Book News*

"…reads well as the author has a very conversational tone, while giving you more than enough information on the topic at hand. He drops in jokes and honest truths, as if you were talking to him in a bar." — *Technology and Me Blog*

Cisco Routers for the Desperate, 2nd Edition

"This really ought to be the book inside every Cisco Router box for the very slim chance things go goofy and help is needed 'right now.'" — *MacCompanion*

"If only Cisco Routers for the Desperate had been on my bookshelf a few years ago! It would have definitely saved me many hours of searching for configuration help on my Cisco routers. . . . I would strongly recommend this book for both IT Professionals looking to get started with Cisco routers, as well as anyone who has to deal with a Cisco router from time to time but doesn't have the time or technological know-how to tackle a more in-depth book on the subject." — *Blogcritics Magazine*

"For me, reading this book was like having one of the guys in my company who lives and breathes Cisco sitting down with me for a day and explaining everything I need to know to handle problems or issues likely to come my way. There may be many additional things I could potentially learn about my Cisco switches, but likely few I'm likely to encounter in my environment." — *IT World*

Absolute OpenBSD

"My current favorite is Absolute OpenBSD: Unix for the Practical Paranoid by Michael W. Lucas from No Starch Press. Anyone should be able to read this book, download OpenBSD, and get it running as quickly as possible." — *Infoworld*

"I recommend Absolute OpenBSD to all programmers and administrators working with the OpenBSD operating system (OS), or considering it." — *UnixReview*

"Absolute OpenBSD by Michael Lucas is a broad and mostly gentle introduction into the world of the OpenBSD operating system. It is sufficiently complete and deep to give someone new to OpenBSD a solid footing for doing real work and the mental tools for further exploration." — *Chris Palmer, President, San Francisco OpenBSD Users Group*

PGP & GPG

"...The World's first user-friendly book on email privacy...unless you're a cryptographer, or never use email, you should read this book." — *Len Sassaman, CodeCon Founder*

"An excellent book that shows the end-user in an easy to read and often entertaining style just about everything they need to know to effectively and properly use PGP and OpenPGP." — *Slashdot*

"PGP & GPG is another excellent book by Michael Lucas. I thoroughly enjoyed his other books due to their content and style. PGP & GPG continues in this fine tradition. If you are trying to learn how to use PGP or GPG, or at least want to ensure you are using them properly, read PGP & GPG." — *TaoSecurity*

Networking for Systems Administrators

"There is a lot of useful information packed into this book. I recommend it!"—*Sunday Morning Linux Review, episode 145*

Tarsnap Mastery

Online Backup for the Truly Paranoid

by Michael W Lucas

Tilted Windmill Press

Author: Michael W Lucas
Technical Review: Colin Percival
Copyediting: Aidan Julianna "AJ" Powell
Cover photo: Elizabeth Lucas
Cover design: Bradley K McDevitt (http://www.bradleykmcdevitt.net)

ISBN-13: 978-0692400203
ISBN-10: 0692400206

Tilted Windmill Press

https://www.tiltedwindmillpress.com

For Liz

Brief Contents

Complete Contents

Acknowledgements

Books are not written in a vacuum. For one thing, the author would turn blue and his eyeballs would explode. Unless he had a pressure suit. But it's hard to type in those heavy gloves, so he'd need a custom pressure suit. And a tank of air won't last more than a page or two.

Actually, vacuum-writing might improve many books. The poorly planned ones would certainly be shorter.

But for this book in particular, several people sacrificed their free time so that I wouldn't write only from my own experience. They range from complete novices to Tarsnap masters. Their comments and thoughts helped improve this book immeasurably, and even when I didn't take their advice, they often made me reconsider why I expressed concepts the way I did. They are, in alphabetical order: Navan Carson, Trannie Carter, John Gamble, Josh Grosse, Larry Hynes, Denis Krienbühl, Henry Hagnäs, Frank Moore, Hakisho Nukama, Andreas Olsson, Jason Tubnor, and Scott Vokes.

Thanks also go to Colin Percival, both for creating Tarsnap and for granting me unlimited access to his brain as I wrote this book.

This book's chapters are numbered in octal. Because computers.

Chapter 00: The Backup Problem

Everyone from big organizations to family photographers worries about preserving their precious data in the event of system failures. But time has changed what we worry about.

Most big corporate offices have racks of servers, supported by tape autochangers that perform the daily ritual of copying terabytes of data off vulnerable disks and onto tape. Many people of my generation got their start in IT as a "tape monkey"—they'd begin each day by pulling yesterday's tapes from the backup library and loading the next day's tapes. This critical job required intensive training and a group effort. Even really smart people will eventually screw up simple and logical tape rotation schemes. Fixing those errors requires involvement from large sections of the IT team.

I've worked for more than one firm with more than one room choked with racks and racks of densely packed tapes. Many of these tapes have tidy computer-printed labels that have faded with time. Others have jagged labels hand-scribbled by the over-caffeinated squirrel that the company fired last year. And there's always one label loose in the middle of the floor, the glue failure unnoticed. Restoring data requires locating the correct tapes—which might not be anywhere near each other, labeled correctly, or labeled at all.

Then there's offsite storage. If the organization's offices are destroyed, offsite backups mean that the company might be able to restore critical data and either close down in an orderly manner or perhaps even survive. Many companies exist solely to shuffle backup tapes to and from offsite storage. This involves boxing up the correct physical tapes and cramming returned tapes into their correct spaces on the aforementioned overloaded shelves. Hopefully the backup firm is better at managing tapes than you are. And there's no obvious problem in having a company's groundbreaking research data worth billions protected by a couple of minimum-wage security guards.

I've unwillingly concluded that most technical people aren't any good at managing physical tapes over time. We get totally disgusted and start over, with a nice new organizational system that promises to solve all issues forever, but over time that system degrades into exactly the same maddening morass. Backup tape management requires the attitudes and aptitudes of a fascist thug masquerading as a file clerk.

Then there's tape disposal. Backups contain sensitive, confidential, or possibly damning information. Big companies and government agencies erase or physically destroy worn-out tapes before disposing of them, and even small companies in certain fields must do the same. Mind you, if someone got your organization's old tapes they'd need your backup software and the right hardware to restore them, but it would be possible.

Sysadmins have a really hard time destroying physical tapes, even if they have a government mandate glaring down at them. Is the data on there really unused? Are you *sure*? Destroying those tapes might mean your job, while nobody would notice yet another box of worn-out tapes in the back of the tape swamp. That room is so terrible that only the tape monkeys go there anyway. The risk/benefit calculation is clear; you keep the tapes if at all possible. Even though their presence reduces the odds of finding the tapes you really need.

Ubiquitous bandwidth and cloud services have changed backup management.

Systems administrators are good at managing logical entities like data. We're *really* good at that, so long as we don't have to touch anything but our keyboards. If a company has hundreds of megabits of external bandwidth available, why not send your backups out over the network, keep the backups in an easily searchable and retrievable format, and turn that horrendous tape room into the geek lounge?

More and more organizations run services in virtual environments provided by external vendors, somewhere far removed from their sysadmins. These hosts have access to far more bandwidth than any enterprise could have hoped for even a few years ago. Backing up these hosts over the network makes even more sense.

But network backup carries a whole bunch of new problems with it.

Placing your backup data on the network means that your old data is live. Someone who stole your tapes from an external warehouse would need a bunch of hardware to retrieve your data. Not so with network backup. Even if you use remote offline backup services like Amazon Glacier, a few keystrokes will resurrect your data in a couple hours.

You could run a private remote backup service, but then you must care for all the hardware and infrastructure involved. Part of the point of using an online backup service is that they do that work for you.

Using an external service requires that you trust the provider to handle their backups. That means they must manage their tapes far better than you do. They must take security precautions to protect your data as well as you would, rather than just piling the tapes in a disused warehouse redolent of many generations of rodents. You must choose an external provider who has invested in equipment and people to make backups a non-issue.

Then there are legal aspects. Suppose I own a company that makes widgets with an advanced super-secret process. My company gets a subpoena. Anything entered as evidence is in the public record. Even if I sincerely desire to cooperate fully with the subpoena, I don't want unrelated information about my special widget manufacturing process going into the public record. If my cloud server or backup provider is hit with a subpoena, they'll hand everything over to the court without blinking. It doesn't matter if the service provider has my backups or if they have my live servers, they'll expose my data and *might not even tell me*. To keep my business running, I really need to know if my information goes out under subpoena.

Some backup services do offer encrypted backups. This is a great idea, but not as simple as it sounds. Encryption can expand the size of your data, increasing the amount of bandwidth and space needed to store the backup. And encrypting a backup means adding complexity to recovery.

Encryption comes in many different grades, usually expressed as key lengths and algorithms. Algorithm choice is important—certain algorithms can be easily broken by freely available software, and most sysadmins don't have the expertise to judge how well an algorithm works for their application. But far more important is how well that algorithm is used as part of the whole system. I can get a safe that is guaranteed to resist acid attacks and shelling by tanks, but if I leave it in the back yard with the door unlatched, it's not secure. A mediocre encryption algorithm used well is more secure than a great algorithm used badly. (A great algorithm used well is best.) Some offsite backup services use nearly unbreakable encryption algorithms, but you must trust that the vendor software implements and uses that algorithm correctly. Most online backup vendors do not share their client software source code, so you can't independently verify the encryption is correctly used.

This is where Tarsnap comes in.

Tarsnap

Tarsnap (https://www.tarsnap.com) bills itself as an online backup service for the truly paranoid. The software was designed and written by Colin Percival, one of those infuriatingly smart people who entered university at age 13 and got a doctorate in computing, heavy on the maths. He served for several years as the FreeBSD Project's Security Officer, regularly dealing with difficult security issues.

Colin is smart—but so what? The world is full of smart people. Some of them write backup software. What makes Tarsnap different from its competitors?

First, the source code for the tarsnap client is freely available for public audit. The code is not open source, but you're free to read it. This isn't uncommon, but Tarsnap Backup Inc. offers cash to anyone who finds bugs in the client code, ranging from $1 for cosmetic errors to $2000 for critical errors. The Tarsnap web site contains a list of people who have claimed bounties, and at which level.

The Tarsnap client encrypts all data before it leaves the host. It sends all data as soon as it's encrypted, so you don't have encrypted backup files eating up space on your system.

Tarsnap also performs *deduplication* of backups. Files contain a surprising amount of redundant information, and multiple files contain even more redundancy. A dozen slightly different versions of this book exist on my computer. I have legitimate and important business and craft reasons for keeping a clean copy of the first draft, the reviewed draft, the copyedited draft, and so on. These copies use a lot of disk space, but between them they have a whole shipping container of redundancy.

Tarsnap stores any given block of data only once, even on different backups. The result is massive compression of stored data.

Tarsnap has specific support for backing up filesystem snapshots, like those in ZFS or some versions of UFS.

All of these features are bundled into a surprisingly simple command-line client that closely resembles tar(1) (and all the other programs that have copied tar's command-line options). Tarsnap's command line is much simpler than tar, however. It doesn't need to cover all the different backup hardware or compression options or other weirdness that tar has evolved to handle.

Tarsnap demands you think differently. If you use Tarsnap like you would use backup systems like Amanda or tar or one of the big commercial tape backups, you'll get unpleasant surprises. Tarsnap's features lead to different behavior than most other backup clients. Used correctly, however, Tarsnap can save your organization, your money, and your peace of mind.

Online Backup Security

For backups, security comes down to confidentiality, integrity, and availability. With an online backup service, confidentiality is the big issue. An intruder can capture your data through three channels: by capturing your keys, by capturing data in transit, or by stealing data at the service provider. Tarsnap offers the same answer to all three risks: you have the source code, verify what it does for yourself.

Decrypting your data would require access to your keys. An intruder might capture your key file by breaking into the server, or by compromising the backups of your key. If someone steals a flash drive containing a backup of your Tarsnap keys, that's not the software's fault. Tarsnap itself doesn't send the key file across the network unless you specifically back it up—and even then, it's encrypted.

If someone captures data in transit to the Tarsnap service, they will be able to tell that you're using Tarsnap. If they watch long enough, they can make an educated guess about how much deduplicated data you're uploading. They can't tell anything about the contents of the data, however, as it's all encrypted. You can verify this by reviewing the source code.

Similarly, the Tarsnap service only stores blobs of encrypted data. If someone was to break into the service, they might figure out how much data you have stored. But they can't see what's in those blobs. All of Tarsnap's cryptographic brains are in the client software.

The whole point of Tarsnap's design and code availability is that it removes any need to trust anyone with your data. Everything is provably encrypted before it leaves your computer.

The Tarsnap Service

In addition to the software's robustness, Tarsnap runs the technology parts of its service very transparently. On those rare occasions there's an outage, Tarsnap publicly admits the problem and offers root cause analysis. Sometimes it's the cloud provider. Sometimes it's human error. Tarsnap Backup Inc. might not be the biggest company in the world, but it's certainly honest.

In addition to technical transparency, there's also the question of legal transparency. Tarsnap Backup Inc. is in Canada. It runs on Amazon cloud services, headquartered in the United States. It is possible that either of these business entities could be subject to a government demand for user data, with an accompanying legal demand to not inform the users.

With Tarsnap's design, the lack of legal transparency is not a problem. I would not expect Colin—or anyone—to go to jail to protect my data.[1] As far as I can tell, Tarsnap's design lets Colin fully comply with

---

1   Colin is a small, mild-mannered dude, and probably wouldn't last long in prison. He's kind of the anti-Chuck-Norris.

any legal, quasi-legal, or blackmail-driven demands while simultaneously being utterly, absolutely unhelpful. The point of Tarsnap is that you have no need to trust anyone outside yourself with the contents of your data. Nobody can access your data without your keys—period.

Contents

This book takes you through using Tarsnap, from your first backup, to restoring a destroyed machine, to optimizing Tarsnap for different environments and conditions.

Chapter 0 is this introduction.

Chapter 1, *Tarsnap Essentials*, discusses Tarsnap's essential features and how they work in the real world. Effectively using features like deduplication requires you understand how they work.

Chapter 2, *Installing Tarsnap*, takes you through installing Tarsnap on platforms like Linux, BSD, Windows, and Mac OS X. Working from these examples, you should be able to install on any supported platform.

Chapter 3, *Tarsnap Client Basics*, teaches you the bare bones of using Tarsnap. You'll register machines with the service and run your first backup and recovery.

Chapter 4, *Creating and Managing Archives*, covers running and manipulating backups.

Chapter 5, *Caches and Keys*, discusses how the Tarsnap cache works and how to repair it in the unlikely event that it breaks. You'll also learn how to encrypt your Tarsnap keys, as well as create keys with limited permissions.

Chapter 6 is about *Backup Rotation and Automation*. If you must run backups by hand, you won't run them. Everyone knows this, even if they deny it. You'll learn simple ways of automating Tarsnap backups, including creating new archives and disposing of old ones.

Chapter 7, *Restoring Archives*, covers the intricacies of getting files back out of your backups.

Finally, Chapter 10, *Full Backup and Restoration*, presents a case study of archiving and restoring a database-driven web server.

Let's get going!

Chapter 01: Tarsnap Essentials

Tarsnap lets you encrypt and back up data from Unix-like systems to the Tarsnap service. All of the encryption and deduplication functions take place in the client; the back end is just a giant indexed storage array. You can view, retrieve, delete, and rotate your backups at any time. Tarsnap's back end storage replaces your tape libraries.

If you're seriously interested in the innards of how Tarsnap works, read Percival's presentation "From bsdtar to tarsnap" from EuroBSD-Con 2013. It contains all kinds of detail on exactly how the algorithms work, how deduplication is managed, and contains real math. While I'm glad this information is available, most of us are not qualified to reverse-engineer Tarsnap's behavior from the formulae in the presentation. This chapter takes you through Tarsnap's core functions and features.

Tarsnap Programs

The main part of the Tarsnap stack is the command-line program tarsnap(1). You'll use this program to create, examine, and extract backups from the Tarsnap service. The tarsnap client is designed like a traditional Unix program—it's meant to do one thing and do it well. Tarsnap deliberately shares a lot of features with traditional tar implementations like GNU tar, star, and BSD tar. We'll use `tarsnap` throughout this book.

Tarsnap has additional commands for managing cryptographic functions. The tarsnap-keygen(1) program creates keys for Tarsnap clients, as Chapter 3 discusses. The key management program tarsnap-keymgmt(1) lets you create cryptographic key files for specific functions. Chapter 5 show how to create Tarsnap keys that can only back up a machine, or only destroy the backups. There are also special-purpose programs like tarsnap-keyregen(1) and tarsnap-recrypt(1), used on those very rare occasions when you must replace your cryptographic keys.

Tarsnap uses a configuration file, `tarsnap.conf`. This normally goes in `/usr/local/etc/tarsnap.conf`, but can change depending on your operating system. We'll use this file to configure Tarsnap to fit your needs, starting in Chapter 3.

Finally, the web interface at https://www.tarsnap.com is where you'll manage your Tarsnap account, funding, and key registrations.

Tarsnap Philosophy

Colin Percival still manages Tarsnap Backup Inc., and he runs it the way he thinks a company should be run. This doesn't quite mesh with what most people would consider typical business practices.

Percival believes that pricing should be fair. Tarsnap stores its data on Amazon's S3 service. When Amazon slashed their storage prices in April 2014, Percival passed the price reduction straight through to Tarsnap's customers. Storage prices are only going to fall, and while he surely can't do this every time a key expense gets cut, Percival has demonstrated that he wants to be meticulously fair. More than one person[2] claims that Tarsnap is *too* inexpensive, and that Tarsnap

---

2   Myself included. I've have paid far more for far worse service, and have told Colin to raise his dang prices already. But that's his decision, not mine.

Backup Inc. needs to increase their rates. Colin holds prices where he considers the service "sufficiently profitable."

Tarsnap operates transparently. There's the bug bounty, which pays cold hard cash for errors in the code. But where most "cloud services" deal with short outages by pretending that they never happened and that any problem must have been on the client side, Tarsnap publicly acknowledges even trivial outages on the user mailing list and Twitter. Customers get an apology and a root cause analysis. While it's impossible for an outsider to say if someone has learned from their mistakes, the only root cause Tarsnap has given more than once is variants on "Amazon broke."

Finally, the transparency extends to security problems. Nobody can completely prevent problems: once vendors achieve a certain grade of security competence, the only thing that separates one from another is how they react when the inevitable issues are discovered.

In January 2011, Taylor R Campbell found an error in the Tarsnap code. This bug meant that it was possible someone could decrypt Tarsnap data stored on the service. Percival reacted by acknowledging the bug and releasing a fix. He credited Campbell publicly, launched the formal bug bounty program, and retroactively sent Campbell a considerable bounty payment. Customers were offered credits so that they could download and re-encrypt all their data, eliminating the risk of future disclosure. He then gave a realistic assessment of the risks caused by the bug, who would be affected, and who should be concerned. Many much larger firms do less, only when forced to or shamed, and even then only grudgingly.

Tarsnap Target Users

Tarsnap is meant for Unix system administrators and developers. It's clearly not designed for casual users of consumer operating systems.

While you can run Tarsnap on Windows (via Cygwin) or OS X, your average construction worker or grocer isn't going to use Tarsnap. People who run a Unix variant other than OS X on their laptop shouldn't have much trouble with it, however.

Tarsnap is designed like a traditional Unix command-line program. While add-on GUIs have been written, these GUIs merely assemble your selections into the corresponding Tarsnap command line.

Tarsnap's most obvious use is for servers, which tend to contain the most irreplaceable data. Many servers specifically require encrypted backups, such as those used in finance, health care, or certain legal arenas. Many people use Tarsnap for personal systems, though, and it works well for them.

Using Tarsnap requires a commitment to maintaining your machine. No cryptography system is perfect, and in the event of a cryptographic compromise you must upgrade your Tarsnap software to the latest version. If you plan to set up a machine and never *ever* touch it, then Tarsnap is not the right backup program for you.

Tarsnap Support

Tarsnap has the traditional support model used by many Unix programs: a low-volume mailing list for user questions. Get information on the mailing list at https://www.tarsnap.com. If you have questions about Tarsnap usage, it's worth searching the mailing list archives. Many questions have been asked repeatedly there, and you'll find detailed answers. If the answer isn't in the archives, subscribe and ask your question. Many experienced Tarsnap users happily help new users with problems, and Percival joins in with information and suggestions.

If your problem involves the back end of the Tarsnap service, such as issues with your Tarsnap account or changes not supported by the

Tarsnap web interface, contact Tarsnap support at support@tarsnap. com. Tarsnap can provide some information not in the web interface.

Tarsnap questions are best handled by the public mailing list— preferably, by searching the mailing list archives for your answer. IRC users can visit the #tarsnap channel on EFnet.

Tarsnap and Organizational Security

People routinely request assistance from Tarsnap Backup Inc. in sneaking Tarsnap data streams out of their network. If you don't want your employer to know you're using Tarsnap, then you probably shouldn't use Tarsnap.

The word "secure" does not mean "invisible." Tarsnap is designed to let an organization back up its data securely by communicating with the Tarsnap service on a well-defined TCP port (9279). It is not designed to bypass organizational security requirements.

Much of the advice in this book is intended to help you minimize the impact of off-site network backups on your infrastructure. This isn't intended to help you evade detection. While you can certainly run Tarsnap over a VPN, Tarsnap is not designed to exfiltrate data from a network.

Tarsnap Backup Inc. cannot help you evade detection. The tool isn't designed that way. While a packet sniffer can't identify the contents of the traffic, the first page of Google's search results for "tcp port 9279" contains several Tarsnap links. Most other search engines give similar results.

If you're trying to identify Tarsnap traffic with a packet sniffer, most of the data looks like random garbage. The initial protocol handshake is recognizable when the Tarsnap service and client exchange protocol numbers. This was a deliberate design decision, to help network engineers identify and understand the traffic. Also, the response to a "store this block" message is always a 135-byte TCP segment. Finally, the server sends an RSA-PSS signed DH parameter that the crypto geeks among you could verify.

Supported Operating Systems

Tarsnap runs on any vaguely modern Unix-like operating system, including but not limited to the various BSDs, Linux, OS X, Open-Indiana, and even Minix. You can run it on Windows using Cygwin. Tarsnap doesn't necessarily support all features of those operating systems, however.

Many operating systems have special filesystem attributes. Apple's HFS+ filesystem, for example, includes extended attributes and deprecated but present resource forks. Extended attributes covered by file flags or POSIX.1e Access Control Lists should work fine with Tarsnap. Those resource forks won't. You can back up the files just fine, but you won't get the special attributes.

Tarsnap gets its support for special filesystem features from libarchive (http://www.libarchive.org/), a toolkit for reading and writing various backup formats. Tarsnap includes a copy of libarchive. If you want to know exactly what filesystem features a version of Tarsnap supports, check the documentation for the included version of libarchive.

Newer versions of libarchive do support HFS+ resource forks. When Tarsnap updates its version of libarchive, it will grow that support. There will always be a gap between what libarchive supports and what people have deployed out in the real world.

The Tarsnap Service Architecture

Tarsnap runs entirely on Amazon's AWS cloud service, accessible to the public on TCP port 9279. When this book was published, the front end ran on a single instance on Amazon's highly-available infrastructure. Tarsnap will add more front end hosts as the userbase grows.

The node you connect to is a FreeBSD system hosted on Amazon's AWS. The server running the Tarsnap front end doesn't do anything with encryption—the client has already done all the encryption. This server primarily accepts client connections, collects accounting information, and feeds lumps of encrypted, deduplicated data to Amazon's Simple Storage Service (S3).

Tarsnap stores your data on a log-based filesystem built atop S3. Most filesystems are designed for flexibility, which increases their complexity. Tarsnap doesn't need a flexible filesystem; it needs a very reliable filesystem that only handles files from 296 bytes to 256kB. These files don't need file names, or permissions, or any of the other features you'd expect from most filesystems. Tarsnap only needs an index system to determine which files belong to which clients. All of the metadata, indexing, and supporting information is held on the EC2 virtual node, but if that node was destroyed the replacement could rebuild the metadata from the filesystem log.

Amazon has less expensive data stores than S3—notably Amazon Glacier, which moves data to near-line storage and can recover it within a few hours. It might seem that Glacier would be a good choice for Tarsnap's back end, especially for older backups. Off-line storage is incompatible with deduplication, however. One block of data might be referenced by dozens or hundreds of backup archives, or many times by a single archive. A block of stored data that hasn't been altered in years and looks ripe for off-line storage might be vital to last week's archive.

Tarsnap has tools to verify the underlying data store and reduce the risk of bit rot. Amazon S3 has its own replication and checksum-based verification, giving the bottom layer of redundancy. Tarsnap itself uses cryptographic signatures on top of S3's error correction, to verify the integrity of any given block of data.

Occasionally someone asks if Tarsnap has considered moving its back end off of Amazon, or to servers outside the United States. While it's possible, it's not likely. Tarsnap is built atop Amazon's S3 programming interfaces. Changing back ends would require a substantial amount of development and testing. For those concerned about data theft from the back end, Tarsnap is designed so that it doesn't matter if anyone steals your encrypted backups. Without the keys on your machine, the backups are useless.

Could the National Security Agency or another national intelligence agency see that you're using Tarsnap? Probably. But intelligence agencies tap intercontinental fiber exactly like they tap in-country fiber. Moving Tarsnap storage to another country only changes which tapped cables your connection uses. Plus, you must somehow pay Tarsnap Backup Inc., and intelligence agencies everywhere devour credit card transaction data. Bitcoin is slightly more anonymous, but not much. Hosting the service outside the United States wouldn't change anyone's visibility into your Tarsnap use.

Tarsnap is designed specifically so that you don't need to trust Tarsnap Backup Inc. or Colin with the contents of your data. If someone was to snoop on Tarsnap data as it crossed the wire, they wouldn't get anything useful. Your least favorite spy agency could collect all of your data from the Tarsnap data store, and it would tell them… precisely nothing about the contents of the data. Thanks to Tarsnap's log-structured filesystem they might figure out how often you run backups and how much new deduplicated data you generate, but that's about it.

The real brains of Tarsnap exist in the client and requires your private key, which resides only on your system.

Tarsnap Core Features

The core features of Tarsnap include encryption, deduplication, archiving, and snapshot support. While these all sound great, the way they work is sometimes non-intuitive.

Encryption

Tarsnap transparently encrypts everything, using a combination of standard encryption algorithms and checksum methods. Tarsnap does not use the common certificate-based SSL to connect to the server. Instead, the Tarsnap server's public key is hard-coded into the Tarsnap client, so Tarsnap can use a simpler protocol than SSL. It also prevents man-in-the-middle attacks. In the event that the Tarsnap private key is ever compromised, you'll need to update your client software.

Crypto fans probably want to know that Tarsnap signs and encrypts most data with multiple 2048-bit RSA keys, but also uses AES-256 keys in certain places. It provides integrity via HMAC-SHA-256 checksums. Tarsnap encrypts not only the archive files, but also the names of the archive files.

While choosing a key length is a common part of creating an SSH key, an SSL certificate, or most other cryptographic processes, Tarsnap doesn't let you select any of these. Tarsnap hard-codes its cryptographic settings. Selecting the proper cryptographic algorithm and key length for an application requires a deep understanding of both the application protocol and the cryptographic algorithms. Tarsnap is a specific application that transmits files of a narrowly limited range of sizes. This lets the software designer choose the best cryptographic algorithms for the purpose.

Many systems administrators believe that longer keys are more secure. Common math says that a 4096-bit RSA key is far tougher to crack than a 2048-bit RSA key. Why would Tarsnap use shorter, more vulnerable keys?

Because cryptography is not common math.

It's true that 4096-bit RSA keys are much tougher to crack via mathematical factoring. But nobody attacks even 2048-bit keys via mathematical factoring. The longest key factored today was 768 bits, and that required two years of real time on a whole bunch of computers. The difficulty of factoring a 2048-bit key is insurmountable today.

If you can't factor the key, how do you attack it? You go around the other way, and attack the implementation: a *side channel* attack. The Tarsnap code carefully avoids a variety of timing and other side channel attacks.

Even if the Tarsnap stack was utterly immune to all possible crypto attacks (which no piece of code is), your operating system probably isn't. But Tarsnap relies on the operating system for core functions like entropy (randomness), networking, basic shared libraries, and such. An operating system flaw impacts Tarsnap's security. If your operating system has poor randomness, then your keys are vulnerable to attack.

When an attacker attacks via side channels, longer keys are often more vulnerable to side channel attacks such as timing attacks. With Tarsnap's protocol, using the RSA algorithm, 2048-bit keys strike the best balance between factorial security and side channel security.

Deduplication

Lots of files have content in common. Databases repeat data. Text files, like logs, repeat data. Even programs have common data in them. And every single shell script starts with #!/bin/sh.[3] Most backup programs store multiple copies of this common data, making the backups even more redundant.

---

3   Or #!/bin/bash, if you're wrong

Tarsnap conserves backup disk space by only backing up information once and keeping an index of where it's used. *Deduplication* can massively reduce the amount of disk space a backup requires, at the cost of increased backup complexity. Deduplication technology is well understood these days, so the added complexity isn't so much of a burden. Deduplication effectively transforms full backups into incremental backups. Tarsnap even deduplicates the vast majority of your metadata. The result is smaller backups without losing any information from any files.

Tarsnap chunks data into blocks, and deduplicates based on the blocks. These blocks do not have a fixed size, allowing Tarsnap to quickly adjust to changes in the middle of a file. The average block size is about 64kB.

The deduplicated blocks are carefully indexed, listing which backup archives use which blocks. When you remove archives, blocks that are no longer needed are removed from the service. Blocks needed by other archives are retained.

Deduplication conflicts with compression. File compression works much like deduplication, but is less efficient than true deduplication. You cannot effectively deduplicate what's already been compressed.

What's more, compression actively interferes with deduplication. Suppose you have a text log file that grows every day. You compress a copy of it every night, and back up the compressed copy with Tarsnap. The compressed backup will take up far more space than you might expect. Yesterday's compressed file will be completely different than today's compressed file, as compression algorithms pull a bunch—but not all—of the redundancy out of the file. The compressed files will be roughly the same size, and expand to similar data, but the compressed files themselves have very little or nothing in common.

This problem has existed for years when combining rsync with gzip. If you're compressing files with gzip, the `--rsyncable` option helps with this problem but doesn't eliminate it.

Generally speaking, don't compress files you want to Tarsnap. If you're backing up your database, run tarsnap on the raw text backup files and not the compressed versions. If you're backing up a SVN repository, back up the uncompressed repository. You probably want to use application dumps or filesystem snapshots to ensure coherent backups, as Chapters 4 and 6 discuss.

Tarsnap can effectively archive static, unchanging compressed files, like compressed man pages. They won't gain much benefit from deduplication, but you'll have a single source of truth for your backups. Many of these files are part of the operating system, however. There's little reason to back up the operating system with Tarsnap, as restoring a machine from a Tarsnap backup requires a base operating system install.

Deduplication is performed on a per-key basis. Tarsnap assumes that each machine you back up has a unique key. It is possible to share one key between multiple machines, letting you deduplicate between machines, but this requires careful automation. In most cases you're better served by thoughtfully selecting what you back up. We'll discuss deduplication between machines in Chapter 5.

Archives

You'll keep hearing the word "archive" around Tarsnap. In conventional backup software, an archive might be a tape set, a tarball, a set of optical disks, or any other storage media. Deduplication fundamentally changes archives in Tarsnap.

In Tarsnap, an *archive* is a named set of deduplicated blocks. The archives live on the Tarsnap service, encrypted with the host's key. Each archive created by a given key has a unique name. Your web server might have archives named "Monday Backup," "Tuesday Backup," and so on. Just like a traditional backup, these archives contain files—and yet, they don't.

In a traditional backup, an archive contains the actual files being backed up. Look at the tape, you'll see the files. In Tarsnap, an archive lists all of the unique data blocks. When you create a new archive, Tarsnap checks for data blocks identical to those that already exist on the service. The client creates a list of all the blocks in the archive, but uploads only the list and the new blocks to the service.

Suppose you have two archives that contain mostly identical data. The two archives together take up two gigabytes on the Tarsnap service. You delete one archive. In conventional backups, this would free up about half the space, or about one gigabyte. When you delete a Tarsnap archive, you delete any data blocks unique to that archive, and then the list of blocks in that archive. We already said that the two backups are mostly identical, so deleting that one archive won't free up much space.

It's sometimes useful to think of an archive as a list of blocks, and sometimes it's useful to think of it as the actual bunch of files. It all depends on how you're using Tarsnap at the moment.

Each archive needs a unique name. If you really name an archive "Monday Backup," you must either give next Monday's backup a new name or delete the old backup before creating a new one. Many people avoid this issue by appending dates or timestamps to archive names.

While archives benefit from deduplication, only needing to store data one time, each archive is an independent thing. Deleting an archive means deleting the list of deduplicated blocks, not the blocks themselves. Tarsnap tracks which blocks belong in which archive. Data blocks are removed only when no archive uses them. Deleting an archive has no effect on data stored in any other archive. A deduplicated block no longer needed by any archive is automatically deleted from the Tarsnap service.

Snapshots

A rapidly-changing filesystem poses backup challenges. If you're using snapshots, you want the backup to represent the filesystem at a specific instant, rather than the files as they existed across a few seconds. Filesystems like UFS and ZFS can create snapshots that represent the state of a filesystem at an exact moment. Linux variants use LVM snapshots, which are less efficient than filesystem snapshots but work on any filesystem. Tarsnap can back up a mounted filesystem snapshot, but you must explicitly notify Tarsnap that you're backing up a snapshot.

Tarsnap uses file modification times to see if it needs to inspect and back up a file. Modification times (mtime) have a granularity of one second. While some platforms include mtime alternatives that have microsecond resolution, they still support the standards-defined mtime. Within that single second an operating system can modify a file, create a snapshot, and modify the file again. The snapshot contains only the first set of file changes.

The first backup of this snapshot contains the first set of changes. Eventually you'll create a new snapshot for backups. If the file in question hasn't changed again, the modification time won't have changed. Tarsnap can't know that it should check for changes to that file. Informing Tarsnap that it's running on a filesystem snapshot lets it check for this error.

Tarsnap works on the contents of files, not on the mount points. When you mount snapshots by date or some other variable scheme, Tarsnap still deduplicates the files and let you restore them to a location of your choosing.

We'll go into more detail on snapshots in Chapter 4.

Tarsnap Privileges

Most people use Tarsnap to archive privilege-protected files—essentially, files readable only by the root user. Tarsnap must run as root to read these files.

If you don't want to run Tarsnap as root, you can't back up files readable only by root. You'll need to change where you store the Tarsnap key. Also be aware that the root user can see all of your Tarsnap configurations, or could log in as you and see your Tarsnap files. You might not trust Tarsnap with your root account, but you must trust your root account with Tarsnap.

Tarsnap Pricing

Tarsnap uses metered pricing, charging one fee per byte stored each month and a separate fee for each byte of bandwidth used. You pay for exactly the storage and bandwidth you need. While the rates are subject to change, they're measured in picodollars (10^{-9} dollars).

Why picodollars? First and foremost, a gigabyte is not an exact unit of measurement. Operating system designers and sysadmins calculate a gigabyte using base 2, while disk manufacturers and network engineers use base 10. The International Electrotechnical Commission name for the base 2 gigabyte is a *gibibyte*, while the word *gigabyte* is reserved for the base 10 unit. The word gigabyte is commonly used for the base 2 measurement, however. By pricing Tarsnap services in a base 10 dollar unit per byte, it's absolutely clear that Tarsnap uses the base 10 gigabyte.

At this book's publication time, Tarsnap's base rate is 250 picodollars per byte stored per month, and 250 picodollars per byte of bandwidth. This works out to $0.25 per base 10 gigabyte per month of storage, and $0.25 per gigabyte of bandwidth. If you send one gigabyte of data to Tarsnap in a month, you'll be charged $0.25 for disk space and $0.25 for bandwidth. Restoring that same data from backup costs $0.25 in bandwidth.[4]

Deduplication slashes the amount of data you back up. Many users have archives totaling multiple terabytes of data, but deduplication reduces that to a few gigabytes. My mail server has 150GB of data backed up, but it's deduplicated down to 5.5GB. It's impossible to predict how any one data set deduplicates. Everybody's data, and their updates to that data, differs. Even comparing similar, simple applications isn't informative—my Wordpress site deduplicates at a different rate than yours thanks to its mix of text and images, and I create new content at a different rate than you do. Saying that my web site generates a few kilobytes of Tarsnap data per week says nothing about what will happen when you Tarsnap your web site. Tarsnap's dry run mode (Chapter 4) computes how well your particular data set deduplicates, but that changes over time.

One place where Tarsnap's pricing might look weird at first is when you look at the daily storage cost in the web site interface. Tarsnap storage is priced in picodollars per month. Different months have different numbers of days, creating a varying cost per day each month.

Tarsnap.com Accounts

You must have a tarsnap.com account to use Tarsnap. The account interface is similar to all of the other web-based services you're familiar with, but we'll walk through the basic functions.

Start by creating an account. Go to https://www.tarsnap.com and ignore all of the technical information about the Tarsnap stack. Click on the "Accounts" tab.

---

4   Percival considered making Tarsnap services cost 12 attodollars per bit-second, but he decided that would be too much work to track.

Creating an account requires an email address and a password, just like any other web service. There's the usual "I agree to the terms and conditions" checkbox. The unusual thing is the "Are you a resident of Canada?" radio button. Tarsnap Backup Inc. is a Canadian company, and customers outside Canada are not subject to Canadian tax rules. Once you create an account you'll get a confirmation email. Click on the link in the email to activate your account.

Be sure that the email account exists before you try to create your Tarsnap account. If the first registration email bounces, Amazon silently drops all further email to that address.[5]

The core functions of the web interface include managing finances and viewing activity on your account, on specific machines, or on all of your machines. You'll also see links for the usual account management functions like changing your password and logging out.

If you need to make changes or gather information not offered in the interface, contact Tarsnap support. They might ask you for more information to double-check that they're taking the correct action. For example, when I needed a defunct machine's archives deleted, they asked me for the exact size of the archive I wanted removed. Tarsnap Backup Inc. really doesn't want to delete the wrong archives!

Account Funding

You pay for Tarsnap service in advance. The $5 minimum payment suffices to run many backups for quite a while. I backed up my web sites (including the site files and a daily Wordpress database dump) with Tarsnap for several months at a total expense of less than forty cents. When you log into your account, you'll see your current account balance on the top of the page.

---

5   Not that I forgot to create my Tarsnap-specific email address before registering. Heavens, no.

Tarsnap accepts payments via PayPal, credit card, and Bitcoin. Bitcoin rates are translated into US dollars. Credit cards are processed by Stripe (who are also vocal Tarsnap customers and advocates). Tarsnap is located in Canada, and US credit cards often charge a foreign transaction fee for Tarsnap payments. Using PayPal or Bitcoin avoids that surcharge.

So long as your account balance is positive, you can register machines and create archives. If the backup you're currently running causes your account to go negative, the backup in process will complete. If your balance goes to zero or negative, you'll get error messages like *Cannot register with server: Account balance for user wossname is not positive.*

By default, Tarsnap Backup Inc. only invoices people in Canada. Non-Canadians who need invoices should contact Tarsnap support. Canadian law requires that Canadian companies send invoices to Canadians. (Canadian law also requires sales tax, which Tarsnap pays out of customer fees.)

Running Out of Money

Tarsnap Backup Inc. charges daily for stored data. If your account balance ever falls below seven days of storage fees, Tarsnap sends you a notification email.

If your balance hits zero or goes negative, you'll get another notification and lose access to your Tarsnap archives. You won't be able to recover archives or create new ones. If your account has a negative balance when you run tarsnap(1), you'll get an error saying that your account is empty and you need to add money.

If your account balance remains below zero for seven days, your archives are deleted.

Watch your account, and your email! Don't let the balance get low. Send Tarsnap some extra cash before you embark on that month-long Internet-free backpacking trip.

Account Activity

Tarsnap provides three separate views on your account: all activity, a specific machine, or all machines.

One thing to note is that the word "machine" is something of a misnomer here. The word machine actually means a key. Tarsnap was written with the assumption that each machine will have its own key, and only one key. People have used one key across multiple machines, as we'll discuss in Chapter 5. You could even use multiple keys on one machine.

The *all activity* display is of financial interest. It displays your daily balance, how much storage and bandwidth you're using, and the amount you've been charged for each of the last 60 days. This report does not list the systems generating those charges. You can give this report to your accountant, although they'd probably prefer you request an actual invoice.

The recent activity for an individual machine report shows how much storage and bandwidth that specific machine (or, rather, key) is using, and the daily expenses.

To see all of your machines together, and the daily Tarsnap utilization for each, view the recent activity for all machines report.

You can download all Tarsnap reports in CSV format.

Now that you have an idea how Tarsnap functions and how the stack fits together, let's install Tarsnap on real machines.

Chapter 02: Installing Tarsnap

Tarsnap runs on Unix-like operating systems and in environments with standard Unix features, like Cygwin. The Tarsnap client is intended to be installed from operating system vendor package or source code. Tarsnap Backup Inc. doesn't offer pre-built binaries for any operating system, although they might in the future.

In a world of ideal security, you would only trust code that you had personally audited for correctness. You'd evaluate everything from the hardware firmware to the compiler to the shell. This stopped being possible decades ago. Today, the best you can do is reduce the number of entities you must trust.

Using Tarsnap demands you trust Tarsnap Backup Inc. The Tarsnap stack is designed to conceal your data from the corporate part of that stack. One reason the client is open is so that the Tarsnap organization needn't offer any legal guarantee that they won't disclose your data. You can personally verify (or have someone else verify) that they lack all ability to disclose your data. Tarsnap could disclose your encrypted blocks, but doesn't know how they fit together. You still must trust that Tarsnap Backup Inc. will maintain good relationships with their back end provider, that they won't delete your data on a whim if you insult Percival's choice of footwear, and so on, but that's a different sort of trust. If Tarsnap Backup Inc. gets subpoenaed for your information, their answer will boil down to a PayPal account or credit card number, how much data you store, and how often you connect to the service, because that's all they know.

31

You also need to trust the tools used to verify and build the Tarsnap client: the compilers, the system libraries, and so on. While it is possible to subvert a compiler to build trojaned programs (see Ken Thompson's paper *Reflections on Trusting Trust*), it would be a stretch to postulate a compiler specifically written to sabotage Tarsnap. You must also trust your operating system vendor to ship a secure OS.

Many operating systems offer a pre-built Tarsnap package. You have already trusted your operating system vendor, so you might as well use it. Operating systems like CentOS, Debian, and FreeBSD have digital signature systems to verify that a package is legitimate. While it's possible that someone could subvert the operating system build cluster and introduce corrupt packages, such an intruder would prefer to target core system utilities. Why sabotage the Tarsnap package when you can put spies into login(1)?

Tarsnap Package Installations

If your operating system offers a Tarsnap package, use it. The OS vendor's package is at least as trustworthy as the operating system itself.

Tarsnap won't work well without its configuration file, `tarsnap.conf`. It's probably in `/etc` or `/usr/local/etc`. Your operating system package might not install it, however. The Tarsnap source code includes a sample configuration file, `tarsnap.conf.sample`. Some operating systems copy the sample into place as `tarsnap.conf`, while others let you do that yourself. Start with the default configuration file.

Building Tarsnap

Some operating systems don't include a Tarsnap package—for example, OpenBSD has concerns about the possibility of violating the license, so they don't build a package. They do offer a port, which is an easy way to build your own package.

If your operating system doesn't offer a Tarsnap package, you get to build Tarsnap yourself. Building and installing the client isn't difficult, once you have the prerequisites installed. Each Unix-like system has unique methods of installing the required packages, and the packages have different names. I'll take you through setting up the installation environment for CentOS, Debian, FreeBSD, OpenBSD, Cygwin, and Apple's OS X. Given these examples, you should be able to install on any supported platform.

If you want to install Tarsnap on multiple machines, and your operating system vendor doesn't offer a package, I recommend using your operating system's native package building system to create an actual OS package. While maintaining Tarsnap binaries on a single system is easy, packages are much more scalable across multiple hosts.

While Tarsnap's dependencies haven't changed for quite some time, if you have trouble you should always check the Tarsnap web site for updated requirements.

Building Prerequisites

Before installing the Tarsnap client you'll need a modern C compiler like GCC or clang, related utilities like make(1), plus the system's header files as well as header files for OpenSSL and zlib. On Linux you'll need the `ext2fs/ext2_fs.h` header.

You'll need an OpenPGP program, like GnuPG (version 1 or 2) or PGP, to verify the source code integrity. We'll cover how to get these in each operating system's section.

CentOS, Red Hat, etc

Linux variants based on or related to Red Hat Linux already include GnuPG, but you'll have to install the development libraries with yum.

```
# yum install glibc-devel openssl-devel zlib-devel e2fsprogs-devel gcc
```

You're now ready to download, verify and build Tarsnap.

Debian, Ubuntu, etc

Debian-based Linuxes also include GnuPG, but have no development tools. Install them with apt-get(8).

```
# apt-get install libssl-dev zlib1g-dev e2fslibs-dev build-essential
```

Go on to download, verify, and build the Tarsnap code.

OpenBSD

Most BSD operating systems ship with a development environment, but without GnuPG. OpenBSD has packages for both GnuPG 1.4 and GnuPG 2. GnuPG 1.4 has few dependencies, while GnuPG 2 has more features but pulls in more software with it. Install whichever you prefer.

```
# pkg_add gnupg
```

OpenBSD lets you install both versions 1 and 2 if you desire. Version 1 is called gpg, while version 2 is installed as gpg2. If you install version 2, substitute the gpg2 command for gpg throughout this book. The output from the commands should be the same.

Proceed to downloading, verifying, and building Tarsnap.

FreeBSD

The only Tarsnap dependency required on FreeBSD is GnuPG.

```
# pkg install gnupg
```

Now download, verify, and build the Tarsnap code.

Cygwin

Cygwin, the Linux-on-Windows software, ships with almost nothing. I recommend the 32-bit version of Cygwin, as 64-bit Cygwin lacks features I consider vital. You need recent versions of the packages gcc-core, make, openssl-devel, zlib-devel, openssl, and gnupg, plus all of their dependencies.

I recommend creating a `/root` directory in your Cygwin install, so that Tarsnap can use the default private key location. Make this directory accessible only to your user (`chmod 700 /root`).

OS X

For OS X, you must install both GnuPG and the developer tools. Get GnuPG from http://gpgtools.org. The developer tools are available from the App Store. If you try to configure Tarsnap without the developer tools, OS X pops up a friendly note on the console offering to fetch and install them for you.

OS X does not have a `/root` directory. You can either create one, or set an alternate key location. Only root should be able to get into a `/root` directory (`chmod 700 /root`).

OpenSSL

Tarsnap relies on OpenSSL for certain cryptographic functions. OpenSSL has developed a terrible security reputation in the last few years. Alternative SSL libraries like BoringSSL and LibreSSL are implementing a more secure SSL library that's API-compatible with OpenSSL. Some people prefer to use these libraries instead of OpenSSL even though they're not yet complete.

The Tarsnap build code looks for the various OpenSSL headers and links to OpenSSL's libcrypto. If your replacement SSL library provides compatibility symlinks or another way to make the library pretend to be OpenSSL, it should work. If you have a problem, the first thing to do is fall back to a version of Tarsnap built with authentic OpenSSL.

Tarsnap uses only a small part of OpenSSL, and none of the OpenSSL reimplementation teams are touching those features yet. The replacement SSL projects are still in flux. Tarsnap won't include them as an option until they stabilize a little. Use the replacements at your peril.

Download and Verify Tarsnap

Now that you have all the tools you'll need, go to the Tarsnap web site and download both the newest source tarball (`tarsnap-auto-conf-something`) and the accompanying SHA256 hash file (`tars-nap-sigs-something`). You'll need the hash file to validate the integrity of the source code. Get these files to your host.

Perform these tasks as a regular, unprivileged user—not as root.

What is OpenPGP Verification?

Tarsnap is for the "truly paranoid." This means that you really need to make sure that the source code you downloaded is the same as the source code Tarsnap Backup Inc. loaded on their web site. That's where OpenPGP comes in.

Each OpenPGP user has a private key that is used to digitally sign or encrypt files. The user keeps their private key secret. Tarsnap Backup Inc. uses a fresh key each year to sign its source code. OpenPGP provides several cryptographic benefits, but the two we care about are integrity and nonrepudiation.

Integrity means that the file has not been changed since being digitally signed. Someone, Tarsnap Backup Inc. in this case, prepared the file, signed it with their key, and offered it to you.

Nonrepudiation means that a person cannot deny signing the file. Tarsnap Backup Inc. can't claim a file signed with their key is not theirs, as they signed it.

It's possible that someone compromised your downloaded file, either by breaking into the Tarsnap web site, infiltrating your ISP's proxy server, or even breaking into your system. Don't choose the world's most secure backup tool and then skimp on security best practices while installing it! Verify your Tarsnap download.

Verification requires getting the most recent Tarsnap OpenPGP key, using that key to verify the signature on the hash file, and using the hash file to verify the integrity of the code download.

The best way to verify the key is to be an OpenPGP user yourself. If you're not, I highly recommend that you get a private key, gather a few signatures, and attach yourself to the Web of Trust. For more information, see my book *PGP & GPG* (No Starch Press, 2006).

Configuring GnuPG

GnuPG includes the OpenPGP tool gpg(1). If you've never used GnuPG before, run gpg with no arguments. This creates your GnuPG configuration files.

```
$ gpg
gpg: directory `/home/mwl/.gnupg' created
gpg: new configuration file `/home/mwl/.gnupg/gpg.conf'
created
gpg: WARNING: options in `/home/mwl/.gnupg/gpg.conf' are
not yet active during this run
gpg: keyring `/home/mwl/.gnupg/secring.gpg' created
gpg: keyring `/home/mwl/.gnupg/pubring.gpg' created
gpg: Go ahead and type your message ...
```

Hit CTRL-C to terminate gpg.

You now have GnuPG configuration files. Go into your new .gnupg directory and open *gpg.conf* in your editor. Most of GnuPG's default settings are perfectly suitable, but as a new user you'll want to automatically fetch keys from the keyserver. Add or uncomment this entry.

```
keyserver-options auto-key-retrieve
```

If you're an experienced GnuPG user, feel free to retrieve keys by hand.

Verifying the Tarsnap Signature

To verify that you have legitimate Tarsnap code, run gpg with the --verify option on the signature file.

```
$ gpg --verify tarsnap-sigs-1.0.35.asc
```

GnuPG automatically fetches the signing key, computes the signatures, and tells you if the signature was made with the key available on the keyserver. If the signature is good, you'll see a line like this:

```
gpg: Good signature from "Tarsnap source code signing
key (Colin Percival) <cperciva@tarsnap.com>"
```

You'll see more messages after this, because you're a new GnuPG user lacking any attachment to the Web of Trust. (While a good signature could be faked for a new user, you'd need a more sophisticated intruder than usual to give you a bogus good signature.) A good signature means that you can use the code.

If the signature is bad, you'll get a straightforward error.

```
gpg: BAD signature from "Tarsnap source code signing key
(Colin Percival) <cperciva@tarsnap.com>"
```

Do not use Tarsnap code with an invalid signature. Ever. Double-check your GnuPG configuration. If everything in your system looks correct, contact the Tarsnap mailing list and ask for guidance.

When you know that the signature is valid you can make sure that the Tarsnap code you downloaded matches the signature. Take a closer look at the verification output. The second line should have a SHA256 checksum and the name of the file.

```
SHA256 (tarsnap-autoconf-1.0.35.tgz) = 6c9f6756bc43bc22…
```

Double-check that the source code file you downloaded has the same name as that in the signature file—in this case, *tarsnap-au-toconf-1.0.35.tgz*. The long string of hexadecimal characters that follows is the cryptographic checksum of that file. Use your operating system's tools to compute the same checksum for the file you have.

On Linux systems and under Cygwin, use sha256sum(1).

```
$ sha256sum tarsnap-autoconf-1.0.35.tgz
```

On BSD systems use sha256(1).

```
$ sha256 tarsnap-autoconf-1.0.35.tgz
```

On OS X use shasum(1). Safari automatically unzips compressed files when you download them. To verify the source code you must disable this behavior in Safari's preferences first.

```
$ shasum -a 256 tarsnap-autoconf-1.0.35.tar
```

You'll get the file's SHA256 checksum.

Compare the checksum in the signature file with the checksum of the file you downloaded. If they match, you downloaded intact Tarsnap code. You can safely build it.

Building and Installing Tarsnap

Extract the source code from the tarball and run the included configure script. Again, you should do all of this as an unprivileged user.

```
$ tar -xf tarsnap-autoconf-1.0.35.tgz
$ cd tarsnap-autoconf-1.0.35
$ ./configure
```

Some systems, like OpenBSD, have a tar(1) that doesn't do auto-decompression, so you'll need to decompress it separately or add a -z.

Like anything set up with autoconf, the configure script offers all sorts of options and most of them aren't terribly useful. If you're running a system that uses an unusual location for shared libraries or some other odd setting, you already know which `configure` options your platform requires. For most of us, the only Tarsnap build option that's really useful is `--prefix`.

The `--prefix` option sets the root directory for the software installation. Use the prefix to place your Tarsnap installation somewhere that it won't share directories with software installed by your operating system or its add-on packages. Tarsnap uses a default prefix of `/usr/local`, meaning that the programs go into `/usr/local/bin`, the man pages into `/usr/local/share/man`, and so on. This keeps Tarsnap isolated from your base system programs in `/bin`, `/usr/man`, and so on.

If your operating system doesn't know about `/usr/local`, or if your operating system uses `/usr/local` for its own stuff, or if some of the locations Tarsnap uses differ from those your system uses, you probably want to customize your Tarsnap build or your operating system. For example, OpenBSD doesn't use `/usr/local/share/man` for man pages, but rather `/usr/local/man`. You can either edit OpenBSD's man page path or change your Tarsnap build options to put the man pages exactly where you like. The `--help` option of Tarsnap's configure script lists ways to twiddle all of the software paths.

Some operating systems, like FreeBSD, put add-on packages in `/usr/local`. You might want to put Tarsnap elsewhere, then. On systems where I compile a whole bunch of software, or where I'm building software to copy to many different machines, I'll use a prefix of `/usr/local/softwarename`, like `/usr/local/tarsnap`. Set the prefix as an argument to the configure script.

```
# ./configure --prefix=/usr/local/tarsnap
```

The configure script examines the local system, verifies that it has all of the dependencies needed to build the software, and sets up the build environment.

If the configure script ends in an error, you're probably missing a dependency. Double-check the packages needed to build on your operating system. The configure script announces what it's looking for when it fails. You get to figure out which package on your operating system provides the missing file or program. Go back and look at the dependencies for your operating system. Newer versions of Tarsnap could possibly add dependencies, although one of Percival's goals is to reduce the Tarsnap code's size and dependencies.

Once the configure script finishes, build the software.

```
$ make
```

After a successful build, you can become root and install the software. Here I use sudo(8), but you could also use su(1).

```
# sudo make install
```

You should now have Tarsnap installed.

Tarsnap installs a default configuration file as */usr/local/etc/ tarsnap.conf.sample*. We'll cover the configuration file in Chapter 3 and then use it through the rest of the book, but when you're first starting out with Tarsnap, copy the default configuration to */usr/local/etc/tarsnap.conf*.

Theoretically, the configure script checks for every problem that might cause a build failure, but the real world contains far more possible errors than any configure script can anticipate. If the build does fail, read the error message. Build errors usually have obvious causes, such as permissions problems or missing programs. If you get a truly weird build error that makes no sense whatsoever to you, start troubleshooting by contacting your operating system support team with a copy of the last several lines of the build errors. They can help you with most OS-specific problems. If they can't help you, send the same information to the tarsnap-users mailing list and ask for aid. Include the operating system and version you're trying to build on.

Hosts Without Compilers

Many machines shouldn't have compilers or compilation tools, and so you shouldn't build Tarsnap on them. You can still build trusted software and install it on these machines, in a couple different ways.

If you have a package building infrastructure, by all means build your own Tarsnap package. Package-based software distribution is far preferable than the alternatives.

You can also tar up the various Tarsnap files, copy the tarball to the installation targets, and extract it there. If you do this, I recommend installing Tarsnap in its own directory hierarchy, like `/usr/local/tarsnap`, so you can easily upgrade it without touching the rest of your system.

Now let's configure Tarsnap clients.

Chapter 03: Tarsnap Client Basics

Using the Tarsnap client is a lot like using tar(1), except that you don't back up to a tape drive or a file, but to the Tarsnap service. Using the Tarsnap client requires registering machines on the Tarsnap service, setting global configuration options in `tarsnap.conf`, and figuring out what you want to back up. You'll also need to know how to debug tarsnap(1) commands, and the general modes of Tarsnap operation.

Before doing anything with Tarsnap, be sure you have a `tarsnap.conf` file as discussed in Chapter 2. Tarsnap generates lots of errors without a basic configuration.

We'll start with registering machines to Tarsnap.

Tarsnap Machines and Keys

Before you can use tarsnap(1), you must register the machine with Tarsnap. Registration tells the Tarsnap service that archives created on this machine use your account. You must have a Tarsnap account (Chapter 1) before registering machines.

Strictly speaking, you don't register machines. You register cryptographic keys. The registration process creates the keys. Tarsnap was written with the assumption that each machine would have its own set of cryptographic keys. Some people have found that they want multiple registered keys on a single machine, to allow different people to handle different parts of the backup process. Other organizations have decided that they want to use one key across multiple machines, so that they can take advantage of deduplication across their entire network of similar machines. Keys can also have passphrase protection. Chapter 5 covers keys in details.

Each registered cryptographic key creates a separate Tarsnap archival namespace. Say you register the machine *www* and the machine *mail*. On both machines you create an archive named `archive-1`. These archives do not overlap–in fact, each server can only see its own archive files. I recommend not reusing archive names, even between machines, if only so we human operators don't confuse our feeble little brains.

I'll start by assuming that you want to use one key per machine. We'll get into more complex cases later.

Registering Machines

Create a key and register it in one step, with the tarsnap-keygen(1) command.

```
# tarsnap-keygen --keyfile keyfile --user username
--machine machine
Enter tarsnap account password:
```

The default Tarsnap keyfile location is `/root/tarsnap.key`. While you can set the key location on the command line, I recommend either using the default or setting the key location in `tarsnap.conf` to whatever makes sense to you.

The username is your https://www.tarsnap.com username.

The machine name is the name of your machine—or, if you prefer, the name of the key for this machine. This name appears only in the Tarsnap web interface. While you can use the same name for multiple keys, that name appears repeatedly in the web interface. Don't confuse yourself! Use different machine names for every key. If you have multiple keys on a machine, you might try a system like *username@ machine*.

Enter your tarsnap.com password when prompted.

If you're running on Cygwin or OS X, you must either create a / root directory or define an alternate key location in `tarsnap.conf`. I usually create /root, as I think it's a useful thing to have on a system, but that's my prejudice. Feel free to cater to your own.

Here I register my web server *www*, with my username mwl@mwl. io.

```
# tarsnap-keygen --keyfile /root/tarsnap.key --user mwl@mwl.io \
    --machine www
```

This key is now registered with the Tarsnap service, letting me create archives and restore them, charging the transactions to my account.

You can protect Tarsnap keys from the beginning with a passphrase by creating them with the `--passphrased` option. Chapter 5 will cover key passphrases. I'm deferring passphrases while I cover Tarsnap's basics.

Tarsnap Key Files

A Tarsnap key file grants access to archives created by this key. If you need to restore a host's backups, you must have the host's key file. Back up the key somewhere safe, such as several high-quality flash drives, a piece of paper in an OCR-friendly font, or on a secure machine in a different location and on a different network.

Don't use Tarsnap backups as your emergency key backup, either on the host itself or on other machines backed up by Tarsnap. If your organization suffers a catastrophic loss, such as a fire that destroys the entire organization, or an intruder that wipes out your entire virtual infrastructure, you need the machine keys to recover your Tarsnap backups. If the disaster-recovery copies of your Tarsnap keys are in Tarsnap, recovery becomes a chicken-and-egg problem. Flash drives are great, until they fail. And you might not notice a flash failure until five minutes after your servers detonate. Paper in a safe deposit box, in a font easily read by an OCR scanner, is one mostly sound key backup strategy.

Tarsnap Backup Inc. cannot help you recover your data if you lose your key. The only thing they can do is remove the archives created by that key. Too many well-secured copies of your key are better than one too few.

Your First Tarsnap Backup

Chapter 4 will go into depth about creating Tarsnap backups, but let's run a quick backup to verify that your machine is talking to the Tarsnap stack. Pick a small directory on your machine to back up. I'm using /etc, because it's only a couple megabytes. Run tarsnap with the -c (create) flag. Specify an archive name with -f. I like including the date in my archive names. Put the directory you want to back up last.[6]

```
# tarsnap -c -f etctest-2014-12-23 /etc/
Directory /usr/local/tarsnap-cache created for
"--cachedir /usr/local/tarsnap-cache"
tarsnap: Removing leading '/' from member names
                 Total size  Compressed size
All archives      1992426           380554
  (unique data)   1892586           351077
This archive      1992426           380554
New data          1892586           351077
```

The first time you run tarsnap, it creates your cache directory. The cache directory contains deduplication information, as discussed in Chapter 5. It then gathers the files to be backed up and deduplicates them. Tarsnap doesn't store any backup files locally. Rather, tarsnap streams everything to the Tarsnap service as it creates the backup.

---

6   Real Unix software requires you put options first on the command line. Accept no substitutes!

Like most tar programs, `tarsnap` removes the leading slash from filenames. This makes restoring without overwriting existing files easier, and in general reduces the risk of problems created by restoring files.

When the backup finishes you'll get the statistics for this Tarsnap operation. See "Viewing Tarsnap Information" later this chapter.

To list all of the archives associated with this machine's key, use the `--list-archives` flag.

```
# tarsnap --list-archives
etctest-2014-12-23
```

This host's key has one archive associated with it.

Your First Extraction

Now that you have data in Tarsnap, let's get that data back out. Don't extract your backup of `/etc` directly into your `/etc` directory; you might break your server. Run `tarsnap` with the `-x` (extract) flag and specify the archive name with `-f`.

```
# cd /tmp
# tarsnap -x -f etctest-2014-12-23
```

You now have a directory `/tmp/etc`, containing a copy of your `/etc` directory as it was when you backed it up.

Before we get too far into backups, let's discuss configuring Tarsnap.

Tarsnap Configuration Files

You can change much of Tarsnap's behavior by using configuration files. The file `tarsnap.conf` affects how Tarsnap behaves on a system-wide level, while an individual user's `.tarsnaprc` affects how Tarsnap behaves just for that user. While command-line options can define almost any behavior you might want in a single run of the command, if you find yourself always using certain options you'll probably want to set them in the configuration file.

The default configuration file location for `tarsnap.conf` is in `/usr/local/etc`, but your operating system might have packaged it elsewhere. A `.tarsnaprc` file goes in the user's home directory.

The configuration file has two types of settings. Some set a variable to a value, while the mere presence of others triggers a behavior. Here I define the keyfile location in `tarsnap.conf`.

```
keyfile /root/tarsnap.key
```

When running that test backup, `tarsnap` printed archive statistics. An option's presence in the configuration file turns this on, and removing it turns it off.

```
# Print statistics when creating or deleting archives
print-stats
```

Any line beginning with a hash mark is a comment.

Most Tarsnap options can appear in either a configuration file or on the command line. To put a command-line option in the configuration file, remove the leading dashes. For example, the *humanize-numbers* option displays statistics in megabytes and gigabytes rather than bytes. You can list this option on the command line as `--humanize-numbers`, or put the string `humanize-numbers` in a configuration file.

When you have an option set in a configuration file, you can usually override it on the command line. The majority of commands have a `--no` version that turns them off. When you set `humanize-numbers` in a configuration file, you can still print bytes for a single command by adding the option `--no-humanize-numbers` on the command line.

Additionally, a user's `.tarsnaprc` overrides the global configuration file for that user. The system administrator can set an option globally in `tarsnap.conf`, but turn that option off for a specific user in their

`.tarsnaprc`. To set that option for a specific run of a command, enable it with the command line option.

To totally ignore the configuration file, use the `--no-default-con-fig` command line option.

Tarsnap Modes and Key Commands

Tarsnap has five key functions, or *modes*: create, delete, list, extract, and read. While Tarsnap has other commands that relate to these modes or to support systems administration tasks, these five modes are the heart of Tarsnap. Later parts of this book go into detail on each of these, but this quick discussion will orient you.

Create mode makes a new archive. You bundle up a bunch of files, deduplicate them, give the collection a name, and ship it off to the Tarsnap service. Use the `-c` flag to activate create mode.

Delete mode removes an archive from the Tarsnap service. Thanks to deduplication, deleting an archive doesn't necessarily remove all of the blocks in that archive. Deletion removes the named list of data blocks and any blocks unique to that list. Use the `-d` flag to call delete mode.

Listing an archive displays a list of all files in that archive. Use the `-t` flag to trigger list mode.

Extract mode pulls files from an archive and writes them to disk. You'll use this mode to restore from backup. Use the `-x` flag to invoke extract mode.

Read mode pulls the contents of an archive, much like extract mode, but sends them to standard output rather than disk. You'd use this if you want to feed your restore process into another process, like `dd`. If you use read mode without another process, you get a raw tar stream dumped to your terminal. For a human being, reading a raw tar stream is educational but not useful. Use the `-r` flag for read mode.

In addition to the modes, Tarsnap has a couple of key commands and modifiers. Here are the ones we'll use most often.

One useful `tarsnap` command is `--list-archives`. This gives a complete list of all archives stored with the local Tarsnap key.

Many Tarsnap commands work on a specific archive. Specify the archive name with `-f`.

Lastly, the `--print-stats` option gives statistics on an individual archive, or on all archives stored with this key.

These commands and the five modes let you perform most routine Tarsnap operations. Other commands are useful only in special circumstances.

Tarsnap Debugging and Statistics

While Tarsnap is deliberately modeled after popular tar implementations, most tar versions don't provide details on network problems or deduplication. The Tarsnap client includes statistical and debugging options for Tarsnap-specific functions as well as options stolen—er, *borrowed*—from tar. For example, Tarsnap commands support the popular `--version` option to print the program version, as well as verbosity controls. Network debugging and deduplication statistics use their own commands, which we'll discuss later.

Verbosity

Tarsnap commands should never fail silently, but sometimes the error messages are minimal—and the success messages even more so. To generate more verbose output to a mode or command, add the `-v` flag. Many modes and commands have a verbose mode, and the effects vary with the command. Verbosely creating or extracting an archive lists the name of each file as it's processed, while a verbose list of archives adds the archive's creation date.

To eliminate routine warnings and comments, use the `--quiet` flag. Everyone who uses any version of tar is accustomed to warnings like "Removing leading '/' from filenames" and similar. The `--quiet` option eliminates this junk. You can set this in the configuration file. To override the configuration file setting for a single Tarsnap command, use the `--no-quiet` command-line option.

Finally, the Tarsnap client can give more details on network issues with the `--noisy-warnings` option. Tarsnap is tolerant of network issues. When a connection to the Tarsnap service fails, the client waits a few seconds and tries again. If you're trying to debug network issues between your host and the Tarsnap service, `--noisy-warnings` can provide more information.

Statistics

Tarsnap can display how much data you've backed up and deduplicated, either in an archive or in all archives for a key. The `--print-stats` option shows how much data crosses the network and gets stored in the Tarsnap service. Here I show how much information is backed up from a machine.

```
# tarsnap --print-stats
                  Total size   Compressed size
All archives      4501849830        2428764688
  (unique data)    801621284         505394042
```

All sizes are in bytes. Sometimes you need bytes, but most of us want a quicker view of our data. The `--humanize-numbers` option shows statistics in megabytes, gigabytes, and so on. I normally set humanize-numbers in *tarsnap.conf* to make it the default, generating output like this. If I want precise byte counts for a change, I can disable this on the command line with `--no-humanize-numbers`.

```
                 Total size  Compressed size
All archives         4.5 GB           2.4 GB
  (unique data)      801 MB           505 MB
```

The first line shows the total amount of data backed up from this machine, for all archives. It totals 4.5 GB, but once it's compressed the archives shrink down to 2.4 GB.

The second line shows the deduplicated data. That 4.5 GB of data deduplicates down to 801 MB, and further compresses to 505 MB. This machine is using 505 MB of Tarsnap storage to back up 4.5 GB of data. I have several backups on this machine, and using Tarsnap has shrunk the archive size by almost 90%.

Not all data deduplicates well. If you Tarsnap completely non-com-pressible data, such as MP3s, most video files, and many photo for-mats, deduplication doesn't save much room.

The compressed data includes a small amount of per-block over-head. If you have many incompressible files, the overhead can even make the compressed data slightly larger than the uncompressed data. You'll still get the benefits of deduplication between multiple archives of the same data, however, so it's usually a win in the long term.

To see the statistics for a specific archive, give the -f flag and the archive name.

```
# tarsnap -f etctest-2014-12-23 --print-stats
                     Total size  Compressed size
All archives             4.5 GB           2.4 GB
  (unique data)          801 MB           505 MB
etctest-2014-12-23       1.9 MB           380 kB
  (unique data)          1.8 MB           351 kB
```

The first two lines show the totals for all archives, but the last two focus on the specified archive. The archive *etctest-2014-12-23* takes up 1.9 MB, but compresses down to 380 kilobytes. It contains 1.8 MB of non-duplicate data, which compresses down to 351 kilobytes. My initial $5 Tarsnap fee will let me retain this archive for decades.

To view the complete stats on all archives, use the `-f` `'*'` option. Remember the single quotes around the asterisk, to avoid shell expansion.

```
# tarsnap --print-stats -f '*'
```

When you create a new archive and want to get an archive size compatible with GNU tar, use the `--totals` option. For most of us, the Tarsnap-specific statistics are more useful. If you want Tarsnap to always print the GNU tar stats, set `totals` in *tarsnap.conf*. You can override this at the command line with `--no-totals`.

To make all Tarsnap commands print statistics, set `print-stats` in the Tarsnap configuration file. Use the `--no-print-stats` command-line option to override this setting for a specific Tarsnap run.

Archive Details

The `--list-archives` option shows all archives created using this key. If you use verbose mode, you'll see the date each archive was created.

```
# tarsnap --list-archives -v
www-yearly-2014-12-23_21:28:48-vardbbk-mysql    2014-12-23 16:35:54
www-daily-2014-12-25_05:30:01-vardbbk-mysql     2014-12-25 00:30:45
...
```

Viewing the archives uses a small amount of bandwidth. The list of archives is stored on the Tarsnap service, but encrypted with your key.

If Tarsnap was an automobile you could now back it out of the driveway, get on the road, and rear-end a traffic cop on your way to the corner store. Let's dive into making proper, useful backups suited for your environment.

Chapter 04: Creating and Managing Archives

Running a single Tarsnap backup of a whole system isn't difficult. It's also not terribly useful. You need to be able to create archives tuned to your exact requirements. You want to specify what you do and don't back up, sort out why your backups suddenly get larger, and test backups to see what they'll do. You'll also need to understand how your network's bandwidth and latency impacts Tarsnap and how to back up filesystem snapshots.

Before creating archives, be sure you read the discussion of what an archive is in Chapter 1.

You can run only one archive creation or deletion with one key at a time. You can read and extract archives while you're creating or deleting them, however.

Creating Archives

Use the -c flag to trigger Tarsnap's archive creation mode. Archive names can be up to 1023 characters long. The only character you can't use is the NUL byte. Specify the archive name with -f.

```
# tarsnap -c -f homearchive /home/
```

You can only run one backup (or deletion) at a time with one key. While all of your machines can run backups simultaneously, each machine can only create or delete one Tarsnap archive at a time.

If a file path to be added to the archive begins with @, @@, or -, put a ./ in front of it. Don't worry about these files in subdirectories, only in the top of an archive. That means, the following is fine.

```
# tarsnap -c -f weirdarchive home/mwl/@@weirdfilename
```

If you were using Tarsnap from inside your directory, however, you'd need to mark off the file.

```
# tarsnap -c -f weirdarchive ./@@weirdfilename
```

If you're automatically backing up the contents of a directory and files with weird names might appear later, you can use ./ with a wildcard.

```
# tarsnap -c -f weirdarchive ./*
```

I normally back up directories rather than files, which eliminates this issue.

Working Directory

Tarsnap, like tar, runs in your current working directory—the directory your command prompt is in. This is why the earlier examples specify target directories like /etc, /home, and so on with a full path, like so.

```
# tarsnap -c -f homearchive /home/
```

The -C flag tells Tarsnap to use a different working directory. Here I instruct Tarsnap to run from the root directory and work on a file or directory called home (with no leading slash).

```
# tarsnap -c -f homearchive -C / home
```

If you want to get rid of the first part of the filenames in archives, change the working directory. Here I get rid of the leading /var/db/postgres/9.2/, but archive the file or directory data under that directory.

```
# tarsnap -c -f postgres -C /var/db/postgres/9.2 data
```

All the paths in my backup will start with the string data.

Archiving Edges

Remember these things when creating archives.

Tarsnap only backs up files. You cannot archive named pipes or other IPC constructs, and you cannot pipe data into Tarsnap. You could pipe a tar archive into Tarsnap, but that's not terribly useful.

Tarsnap skips synthetic filesystems, or pseudo-filesystems, like /proc, /dev (if the OS uses a device filesystem), and so on. Not only is there no reason to back these up, the contents can fluctuate during the backup. Worse, reading special nodes on certain Linux systems can cause a kernel panic. If you have a really special edge case and you really and truly must back up one of these filesystems, use the --insane-filesystems option. Tarsnap will descend into the filesystem and do its best with whatever weirdness it finds. If you want Tarsnap to always back up these filesystems, you can set insane-filesystems in tarsnap.conf. Override this config file setting with the --no-insane-filesystems option.

When you design your Tarsnap backup strategy, remember that the slowest part of Tarsnap is restoring files. When you restore an entire machine you'll want to run multiple restore processes simultaneously. The easiest way to parallelize restores is to have multiple archives on a single machine.

Listing Archives

We already saw that the --list-archives option displays this key's archives on the Tarsnap service. Verbose mode adds the creation date to each archive listing.

```
# tarsnap --list-archives -v
www-yearly-2015-01-01_01:21:42-usrlocalscripts  2015-01-01 20:28:54
www-yearly-2015-01-01_01:21:42-vardbbk-mysql    2015-01-01 20:26:30
…
```

Tarsnap displays the archives in an arbitrary order. When I look at a list of archives, I usually want to see the oldest or newest archives first. You can use sort(1) to put these in date and time order. Here I list all of the archives in order by creation date. I also use the column(1) command to automatically arrange them as an orderly table.

```
# tarsnap --list-archives -v | sort -ik 2,3 | column -t
```

To sort by reverse chronological order, add the -r option to the sort command.

If you add a second -v, you'll also see the command line used to produce the archive. I'll normally only do this in combination with grep, to see how I created a specific archive.

Tarsnap archive names can include any character. You can even end an archive name with a space. This makes the archive difficult to manage, as the name appears in the list but the trailing space looks exactly like, well, nothing. If you see an archive in the list, but you can't use other Tarsnap commands on it, try running --list-archives through hexdump(1).

```
# tarsnap --list-archives | hexdump -C
```

The display is messy, but it will clearly display trailing whitespace in that archive name. You might need to escape or quote the archive name to extract or delete it.

Viewing Archive Contents

View the files within an archive with Tarsnap's list mode. Use -t to list the files in an archive, and -f to specify the archive name.

```
# tarsnap -t -f 2015-01-0-homemwl
home/mwl/
home/mwl/.mail_aliases
home/mwl/.cshrc
home/mwl/.mailrc
...
```

You can use grep(1), sort(1), and other standard Unix utilities to process the file list.

If you add `-v` for verbose mode, `tarsnap` displays files in Unix "long list" mode, with the file permissions, owners, size, and creation time.

Deleting Archives

Use the `-d` flag to delete an archive. Here I delete the test archive I created in Chapter 3.

```
# tarsnap -d -f etctest-2014-12-23
```

Remember, an archive is a named set of deduplicated blocks. Deleting an archive might not free up much space from the Tarsnap service, depending on which other archives also use the blocks in this archive.

You can delete multiple archives simultaneously by using multiple `-f` flags. This can be faster and use less bandwidth than deleting them in separate commands.

```
# tarsnap -d -f archive1 -f archive2
```

You'll get separate statistics reports for each.

Deleting an archive requires downloading the list of blocks in the archive, so that Tarsnap can figure out which blocks are still needed and which can be destroyed. The deletion request uses an amount of bandwidth roughly equal to 0.5% of the size of the archive. The client then requests that all unneeded unique blocks be destroyed. Depending on the archive uniqueness and size, this can take longer than you might expect.[7]

---

7   Yes, this is vague. Because I don't know your data. My large archive deletions usually finish right after I think "Ah crud, it's hung up."

Deleting All Backups

If you want to destroy all Tarsnap backups for a key, nuke your archives. Much as the name implies, this eradicates everything stored in the service.

```
# tarsnap --nuke
Please type 'No Tomorrow' to continue
```

Enter `No Tomorrow` and Tarsnap loses all the blocks stored with this key. You'll need to start over—which is presumably what you wanted.

Watching Backups

Tarsnap operates quietly unless it has a specific warning to offer. This means that when you run a backup, it doesn't say much. If you gave it an absolute path you'll get a message that says *tarsnap: Removing leading '/' from member names*, but otherwise… silence. Tarsnap is working during that pause, but it has nothing exciting to report, so it says nothing.

You might expect Tarsnap to offer a progress meter, like many other programs. "Progress" in a Tarsnap backup means a whole bunch of different things, though. Are you half done when tarsnap(1) has *read* half of your files, or when it's *deduplicated* half your files? Or maybe when half of your deduplicated blocks are uploaded? Different archives have different bottlenecks. Thanks to the way Tarsnap works, some of these would generate non-intuitive feedback—for example, deduplication doesn't occur until shortly before the block is uploaded. You might create and upload a whole bunch of blocks at the beginning of the archive, then just count those same blocks over and over again. Any Tarsnap progress meter would make those in commercial operating systems look sensible and trustworthy.

If you're trying to figure out what Tarsnap is doing, or you just want it to print something so that you know it hasn't fallen over and died, tell it to be noisy with the -v option. The output still pauses as Tarsnap processes large or nondeduplicatable files. In verbose mode, Tarsnap prints each file's name when it starts working on the file.

If you didn't use -v, but you still want to see what Tarsnap is processing, in a separate terminal send SIGUSR1 or SIGINFO to the running tarsnap process. BSD users can hit CTRL-T to generate a SIG-INFO.

```
# pkill --signal SIGUSR1 tarsnap
```

The running Tarsnap window will print a message like this.

```
adding home/mwl/tcpdump-4.6.2/libnetdissect.a (3080192 /
6117258)
```

In this case, Tarsnap is working on filesystem block 3080192 of 6117258 of the file *libnetdissect.a.*

Dry Runs

Tarsnap can perform *dry runs*, letting you see what would happen if you ran a command, but without making any changes or communicating with the Tarsnap service. Use the --dry-run option to see how configuration changes would alter backups or to display what files Tarsnap would restore.

A dry run shows --print-stats output for this hypothetical Tarsnap backup. It gives you a good idea how deduplication affects your backup and how much new data this operation would send to the Tarsnap service.

If you want to know which files it would include in the archive, use the -v flag.

```
# tarsnap -cvf complete-2014-12-28 --dry-run /
```

Wouldn't this show every file on the system? Pretty much, unless you've deliberately excluded some.

Including and Excluding Files

You probably have files you don't want to back up. The various temporary directories jump immediately to mind. Each system has entire directory hierarchies that don't need backing up. Some operating systems have directories that don't need backups, like `/var/cache` on CentOS and `/var/spool` on BSD.

Many sysadmins treat operating systems installations as disposable, and only care about the data housed on those systems. These sysadmins specifically want to never back up operating system files, only the application data. Others have directories of easily-reproduced data. I keep dozens of operating system installation ISO images on my laptop, and while they're convenient to have at hand I certainly don't want to back them up to Tarsnap!

Tarsnap has *include* and *exclude* options that let you target specific directories for backing up and exclude other directories from being backed up. This lets you run a "full backup" that specifically excludes certain parts of the system. You can also exclude core files, temp files, and other ephemera. These options often appear in a configuration file, but also have uses on the command line. We'll start by using configuration file examples.

include

Tarsnap defaults to letting you back up the entire system. The presence of an `include` option in `tarsnap.conf` reverses that default, so that you can only back up explicitly listed directories.

```
include /home
include /var/log
```

These two options, without any other `include` or `exclude` directives, tell tarsnap(1) that it can only back up files in these directories. If you attempt to back up a directory other than these, `tarsnap` runs but the results show that your new archive is practically empty.

```
# tarsnap -cf etc /etc
...
                Total size   Compressed size
All archives    192 MB           164 MB
 (unique data)  190 MB           163 MB
This archive    1.4 kB           1.2 kB
New data        1.4 kB           1.2 kB
```

1.2 kB is far too small for a new archive, even with deduplication.

I deliberately did not put the trailing slash on the directories in the `include` statements. If I specified the trailing slash, I'd need to use the slash on the command line as well. I'm human, so I'm by definition forgetful and sloppy. I want Tarsnap to do the right thing even when I fail to be precise.

When you start with the `include` and `exclude` options, verify which files your backup captures by using the `--dry-run` and `-v` options before running an actual backup. A `-v` on the previous command would have shown that the archive contains nothing.

exclude

If you want to back up most of the system except for a few key directories, the `exclude` option is your friend. Here I tell Tarsnap it may not back up two directories.

```
exclude /var/db/cache
exclude /tmp
```

If I run a full system backup, it silently excludes these directories.

Tarsnap processes `exclude` directives before `include` ones. If you exclude a directory, you cannot include a directory beneath it.

```
exclude /home/
include /home/mwl
```

While you might think this says "don't back up /home, except for Lucas' home directory," what it really means is "don't back up /home, period. No, not even when you say to back it up." The reverse would be useful, however.

```
exclude /home/mwl
include /home/
```

This backs up every directory in /home, except for the specified directory.

Matching Includes and Excludes

Includes and excludes are matched as relative paths, not as absolute paths. Consider the following tarsnap.conf entries.

```
exclude /home/mwl/storm
include /home
```

I can back up anything in /home, except the directory /home/mwl/storm. That seems simple enough. Let's back up the whole system and see what happens.

```
# tarsnap --dry-run -cvf homebackup /
```

I'm using --dry-run, as this is a test. The command returns almost immediately, creating a tiny archive. I have gigabytes of data in my home directory. What happened?

Tarsnap compared the directory it was supposed to back up (/) with the directories it's allowed to back up (/home). You didn't request an included directory, so the archive contains only the archive name. To back up the /home filesystem, list that exact path on the command line.

```
# tarsnap -cvf homebackup /home
```

This archive now contains the files from the home directory.

64

The command-line path must match the include statement in `tarsnap.conf`. I specified an absolute path, beginning with a slash (`/home`). This means I must include the absolute path on the command line.

```
# cd /
# tarsnap -cvf homebackup home
```

This archive is also empty. Why? I'm in the root directory. I want to back up `/home`. Being in root and specifying "home" is the same as `/home`, right? Well, no. Tarsnap compared what you asked for (`home`) with what it may back up (`/home`) and concluded that they didn't match.

Excludes are matched as paths, so the directory you run a command from matters. Suppose I try to back up my home directory.

```
# cd /home/mwl
# tarsnap -cvf homebackup *
```

This archive is empty. While I'm in a directory Tarsnap is configured to include, and trying to back up the directory I'm in, the included directory (`/home`) does not match what I'm trying to back up (*). I must specify the full path on the command line.

Similarly, excludes only work if you match the path. Consider this `tarsnap.conf` exclude statement. There are no accompanying include statements.

```
exclude home/mwl
```

So, I can't back up my home directory, right? Uh, not quite. The previous example backs it up just fine. The path given on the command line doesn't match what's in the exclude statement. Now if I had a directory `/home/mwl/home/mwl`, that directory would not get backed up.

In short, include and exclude statements are advisory. You can work around them if you try. If nothing else, command-line options can tell Tarsnap to ignore the configured include and exclude statements.

Wildcards can help work around the limitations of include and exclude statements.

Wildcards

Tarsnap uses an asterisk (*) as a wildcard in include and exclude statements. You can use the wildcard to include or exclude patterns.

I often use wildcards to exclude temporary directories. Over the years I've had to support many operating systems, and many of them stick a temporary directory somewhere I never expect to find one. I don't care where a sysadmin has stuck a temporary directory, I just know I don't want to back it up.

```
exclude *tmp*
```

This prevents Tarsnap from backing up anything with the string *tmp* in its name or path. Like `/var/log/wtmp`, or anything in CentOS' `/etc/tmpfiles.d`. That's a little stronger than I want. Maybe I should add directory separators to my exclude term.

```
exclude */tmp/*
```

This excludes `/tmp`, `/usr/tmp`, `/var/tmp`, `/opt/doofus/tmp`, and whatever other temporary directories might exist on your system. The pattern doesn't match anything that isn't in or under a temporary directory, so your user login log is backed up.

You can also use wildcards to not back up core files.

```
exclude *.core
```

There's no wildcard at the end of the string, so the file must end in with `.core`.

OS X uses a directory in each user's account to cache temporary information. There might be a reason to back up this cache, but I'm not aware of it. Exclude it with a wildcard.

```
exclude Users/*/Library/Caches
```

GNOME users often report problems backing up the .*gvfs* directory in their home directory. GNOME creates this directory, and then sets all sorts of filesystem attributes on it to make it hard to delete. Or back up. Or look at askance. If you lose this directory or change its attributes, GNOME notices and, knowing you wouldn't possibly want to change its settings, conveniently restores it for you. Save yourself pain and exclude it from your backups.

```
exclude */.gvfs/*
```

You'll find other files that give similar reasons to use this feature.

Users Excluding Files

Most users are willing to identify data as "don't back this up" if it means that their important data is reliably backed up. Most Unix filesystems let a user set a *nodump* flag or attribute on a file or directory that indicates the data should not be backed up. While nodump was intended for use with dump(8), Tarsnap checks for and honors the nodump flag if you use the --nodump command-line option or set nodump in the configuration file.

Linux systems call features like nodump *attributes*. Use chattr(1) with the +d option to set the nodump attribute on a file. Here I set nodump on the file *debug.txt*.

```
$ chattr +d debug.txt
```

To check for the presence of file flags like nodump, use lsattr(1). The presence of a *d* indicates the nodump attribute is set.

```
$ lsattr debug.txt
------d--------- debug.txt
```

To remove the nodump attribute, use chattr(1) again but with the -d flag.

```
$ chattr -d debug.txt
```

Tarsnap will now back up the file.

BSD systems call settings like nodump *file flags*. To set nodump on a file, use chflags(1).

```
$ chflags nodump debug.txt
```

BSD's standard ls(1) program shows file flags when you use the `-lo` option.

```
# ls -lo debug.txt
-rw-r--r--  1 mwl  wheel  nodump 5293452 Dec 29 15:35
debug.txt
```

The fifth field shows all flags set on this file.

To remove the flag, use chflags(1) to set the *dump* flag on the file.

```
$ chflags dump debug.txt
```

For Tarsnap to respect these file flags and attributes, you must use the `--nodump` argument. You can also set this option in `tarsnap.conf`. Like most other Tarsnap commands, there's also a `--no-nodump` command-line option that tells Tarsnap to ignore the `nodump` setting in the configuration file.

Excludes on the Command Line

The `--exclude` command-line argument lets you specify a path to exclude from Tarsnap's backup. Suppose I want to back up everything from `/home` except `/home/mwl`. I could list every directory under `/home` except that one, or I could explicitly exclude it on the command line.

```
# tarsnap -cvf fullhome --exclude home/mwl /home
```

The exclude pattern works exactly like an exclude option in `tarsnap.conf`. An absolute path (like `/home/mwl`) can never match a relative path (like `home/mwl`), thanks to the leading slash.

Overriding exclude and include Configurations

Configure `tarsnap.conf` with the exclude and include statements you routinely want, but everybody hits times that aren't routine. Eventually, on one of your servers, you'll run into a situation where you need to back up even the files you deliberately excluded in `tarsnap.conf`. You could change your configuration, but that's annoying and might introduce errors.

Tarsnap's command-line options `--no-config-exclude` and `--no-config-include` tell the Tarsnap client to ignore these statements in the configuration file. You can create your special backup, including stuff you normally wouldn't back up. Be sure you give this archive a special name, so you can easily find and delete it when you no longer need the backup.

Inclusion and Exclusion Files

Tarsnap also lets you read exclude and include patterns from a file. If you have a whole bunch of exclusions or inclusions for a backup, list each on a separate line in a text file and call the text file from the command line.

A sample file might start with something like the list below. The paths here lack a leading slash, as we're processing these exclusions on the command line. (Remember, when you put exclusions on the command line, Tarsnap compares them to the file names with the leading slash stripped.)

```
home/mwl/build
home/mwl/ansible
home/mwl/tmp
home/jkm/junk
home/mwl/irsaudit
home/bcp/iso
home/eap/hamsters
...
```

The file must end with a newline.

To use these as exclusions, call the file with -x.

```
# tarsnap -cf homebackup -X exclusions.txt /home
```

To use them as include statements, call the file with -т.

```
# tarsnap -cf homebackup -T inclusions.txt
```

This saves you from typing a horrific command line, and lets you easily reuse the exclusion list.

Backup Checkpoints

Things go wrong. Internet connections fail, Amazon EC2 goes down screaming in toxic flames, and your pet rat waltzes across your keyboard and demands a treat while a process runs. When you're creating a multi-terabyte Tarsnap backup over a period of days, an interrupted backup can spark well-justified rage.

If you're using Tarsnap on a laptop, suspending or hibernating the laptop interrupts your TCP connection. When your laptop resumes, Tarsnap resumes where it left off if you have connectivity to the Tarsnap service at the new location. The real problems happen with unexpected interruptions.

Tarsnap uses *checkpoints* at regular intervals to record how much it has done and where it left off, so you can easily restart a backup. A checkpoint is a mark in the local cache saying "I've done this much." It's like counting pennies and putting them in paper rolls. If someone interrupts your count, you don't need to start over from the beginning: the rolled coins are safely totaled, and you can start over on the current roll.

The default `tarsnap.conf` tells the client to create a checkpoint every gigabyte of data. The client transmits a gigabyte to the Tarsnap service, creates a checkpoint, transmits another gigabyte, creates another checkpoint, and so on. If the backup is interrupted, it can resume from the most recent checkpoint.

Creating Checkpoints

The checkpoint-bytes configuration file option tells Tarsnap how many bytes to upload before creating a checkpoint. While the default is to create a checkpoint each gigabyte, on a slow link you might want more frequent checkpoints. Here I set a checkpoint every 100MB.

```
checkpoint-bytes 100M
```

You can set checkpoints on the command line, with the `--checkpoint-bytes` option.

```
# tarsnap -cf slowbackup --checkpoint-bytes 100M /var/db
```

As always, command line options override configuration file settings.

If you decide during a backup that you want to create a checkpoint, send the running `tarsnap` process a SIGUSR2 signal.

```
# pkill --signal SIGUSR2 tarsnap
```

Creating a checkpoint uses about a megabyte of bandwidth and takes about thirty seconds. Tarsnap pricing means that the megabyte of bandwidth isn't a huge deal, but the time requirement is. Deciding how often to create a checkpoint requires balancing time versus bandwidth. Creating a checkpoint every hundred megabytes, rather than once a gigabyte, means that for every gigabyte you upload Tarsnap spends about five minutes creating checkpoints, rather than thirty seconds.

Viewing Checkpoints

If you run `tarsnap` in verbose mode, it informs you when it creates a checkpoint.[8]

```
# tarsnap -cvf flamp3 FLA/
...
a FLA/AirMech/03 - Pulse Charge.mp3
a FLA/AirMech/04 - Prep for Combat.mp3
tarsnap: Creating checkpoint... done.
a FLA/AirMech/05 - System Anomaly.mp3
a FLA/AirMech/06 - Mech Killer.mp3
...
```

I hit CTRL-C right here, killing the archive operation. Thanks to the checkpoint created during file 04, I can run this backup again and not have to upload anything before that checkpoint.

Archive Recovery

As part of completing an archive, Tarsnap bundles up the information on the backup, adds the archive name to the list of archives, and performs a bunch of other back-end bookkeeping. Interrupted backups don't get that finalizing treatment. While the incomplete archive exists on the Tarsnap service, it's hidden from the list of archives until you either create or delete a new archive, or until you manually recover it. In normal use you'll never have to recover incomplete archives, but I'm going through it to illustrate checkpoints.

To manually recover a Tarsnap archive, use the `--recover` option.

```
# tarsnap --recover
```

Incomplete archives have *.part* added to the end. Here's the archive created by the interrupted backup shown above.

---

8   Why am I backing up MP3 files? Writing a book about a service means abusing it in every way you can conceive. While archiving easily-reproduced media files is daft, using Tarsnap to protect your lovingly artisan-ripped files might be worth it. Tarsnap Backup Inc. will happily let you pay to archive either.

```
# tarsnap --list-archives
...
flamp3.part
...
```

Do not delete these partial archives until you have a complete archive! They contain deduplicated data blocks useful to a complete archive of the same data.

Let's look at this partial archive and see what it contains. Use -t (list) mode and the archive name.

```
# tarsnap -tf flamp3.part
...
FLA/13 AirMech/02 - Arise.mp3
FLA/13 AirMech/03 - Pulse Charge.mp3
FLA/13 AirMech/04 - Prep for Combat.mp3
tarsnap: Truncated input file (need to skip 9333760 bytes)
tarsnap: Error exit delayed from previous errors.
```

Tarsnap created a checkpoint during file 04, so part of the file is present. Files 02 and 03 are intact. While we watched Tarsnap back up files 05 and 06, they were handled after the checkpoint. Those blocks were not successfully uploaded and archived, and are therefore lost. You'll must re-upload them.

You can pick up almost where you left off, however.

Resuming Interrupted Archives

Tarsnap doesn't "resume" interrupted backups. What you can do is create a new backup of the same files, using a different archive name. Tarsnap won't re-upload the blocks in the truncated upload. You can then remove the incomplete archive. (Remember, a Tarsnap archive is a named set of unique data blocks.)

When you create the new archive, Tarsnap quickly runs through the files you've already uploaded, up until it hits the last checkpoint. The Tarsnap client uploads everything after that last checkpoint to the service.

Once Tarsnap finishes creating the new archive, you can remove the incomplete archive and rename the replacement archive to the desired name.

Manual Checkpoint Creation

Maybe you know a backup is going to be interrupted. Your server is about to crash or the datacenter power is about to die. If you're about to interrupt a backup, but you want Tarsnap to take advantage of all the data you've uploaded and cleanly document the interruption, create a checkpoint as you exit the client.

To create a checkpoint when you manually quit a Tarsnap session, use CTRL-Q (or send SIGQUIT to the Tarsnap process) instead of CTRL-C. The last file is probably still incomplete, but all of the blocks already uploaded are kept. Creating a checkpoint will still take about 30 seconds or so.

If you interrupt a Tarsnap session with CTRL-C, no final checkpoint is created. Completing the archive picks up from the last existing checkpoint.

I usually pretend that CTRL-C does not exist in Tarsnap. Always use CTRL-Q if you can wait the 30 seconds.

Oversize Archives

Sometimes an archive has more data than expected. More than one laptop user reports that while their home directory hasn't changed much, their nightly backups contain dozens or hundreds of megabytes of files. Maybe these files don't need backup, or maybe the user was wrong and those files do need backing up. You can't know which until you identify the changing files.

Tarsnap has no tools for reporting the differences between two archives. You cannot look at a new data block and identify which file that block came from. As Tarsnap converts your data to a tar stream and deduplicates the stream, so some deduplicated blocks contain chunks from several different files.

Use standard systems administration tools to identify new and changed files. Tarsnap backs up files modified or created since the last time you archived that part of the filesystem. Many applications, notably those on end user machines, use scratch files or cache directories. You probably do want to archive your browser's bookmarks and settings files, but the web page cache isn't needed.

Use the find(1) command to identify files that have changed recently. Different find implementations have different ways to express times, so you'll want to check your documentation. Here I find files that have been created or changed within the last 36 hours on a system using BSD-style find(1).

```
# find /home/mwl -mtime -36h
```

Somewhere in the results will be file changes you were unaware of. Do you need those files backed up? Only you can tell. Adjust your exclude and include settings to meet your needs.

Live Files and Snapshots

Most people use Tarsnap on live filesystems. This means that Tarsnap might back up a file as it's being changed. The backup might contain the changes. It might not. A partially changed binary file might not even be usable.

Depending on your use case, backing up a half-changed file might be acceptable. If you're backing up your desktop, you know to run your backup when you're not actively editing files. If you're backing up plain text web server logs, you might lose a line or two if the log writes precisely when Tarsnap reads that file. You probably don't care about these risks. Other files are more tetchy. A couple options to ensure coherent, usable backups include turning live files into cold ones and creating filesystem snapshots.

Making Live Files Cold

Backing up a live database's binary back end files is risky. If the database software touches the files while Tarsnap is running, Tarsnap might copy a file that's half old and half new. This is an incoherent backup. Over the years I've gotten pretty good at repairing damaged MySQL databases, but that doesn't mean I'm looking for opportunities to hone that skill!

Don't Tarsnap live database files. Transform those files into cold, static files. Database vendors all provide utilities for generating backups. Use them. Create plain text database dumps and Tarsnap the dumps.

Don't compress database dumps if you can avoid it, as Tarsnap deduplication is more efficient over time than any compression program. Compression works within a single file set, while deduplication affects all the files ever archived.

While I specifically mention databases here, the same principle applies to any application that creates its own back-end storage. You're the system administrator. You know your applications. If your app does something database-ish, check the documentation for its backup process.

Chapter 10 demonstrates backing up and restoring a database-backed application.

Filesystem Snapshots

Tarsnap can take anywhere from a few seconds to a few minutes to traverse a complete filesystem, depending on the filesystem size and how many files change. While a file might not change as Tarsnap is backing it up, it might change during the backup but before Tarsnap gets to it. If you need a fully coherent backup of the state of all files on the system at an exact moment in time, filesystem snapshots are your friend.

Filesystems like ZFS and BSD's UFS support filesystem-level snapshots, giving you a read-only view of the filesystem as it existed at an exact instant. Most Linux filesystems rely on LVM snapshots, which are less efficient but can work on any filesystem. If you mount a snapshot, Tarsnap can back it up. While the specifics of creating, using, and destroying snapshots on all filesystems on all Unix-like systems is way beyond the scope of this book, we'll cover the basics of using Tarsnap to back up a filesystem snapshot. Backing up from a snapshot makes unusual errors possible, but they're easily avoided if you know how.

What can go wrong with a snapshot? Tarsnap, like most programs performing incremental backups, uses a file's modification time (mtime) to see if the file has changed since the last backup. The modification time changes in one second increments, and a computer can do an awful lot of things in that one second. (Some operating systems offer mtime alternatives that track changes down to the millisecond, but those functions are not standard between operating systems.) The system might modify a file, create a snapshot, and modify the file again, all within that single second. The snapshot contains only the first changes to the file, but the file has new changes put in place after the snapshot was taken—and the file's timestamp has not changed.

When Tarsnap first backs up the filesystem, it archives the version of the file in the snapshot, as you expect. The next time you snapshot the filesystem and back it up, however, Tarsnap won't see that the file has changed since the last time it ran. Tarsnap doesn't back up the newer version of the file.

Avoid this problem by using the --snaptime option. This lets you specify a file modified before the snapshot is taken, usually a file you create specifically for this purpose. Tarsnap knows that any files modified after the times on the file might have changes, and examines them more closely. Use `--snaptime` every time you back up from a snapshot.

While you could specify a file in the snapshot that's a few seconds older than the snapshot, the usual way to define a snaptime file is with touch(1). Here I create a snaptime file for `/home`.

```
# touch /home/snaptime
```

Now use your filesystem's usual tools to create a snapshot of `/home` and mount it on `/mnt`. If you have ZFS or another filesystem that automatically mounts snapshots, use the automatic mount point instead. You can then Tarsnap the snapshot on the temporary mount.

```
# tarsnap --snaptime /home/snaptime -cf home /mnt
```

Once the backup finishes, unmount and destroy the snapshot.

Tarsnap now checks for files changed after the mtime on the snaptime file.

Traffic Shaping and I/O Limiting

A big part of system administration is adjusting system limits to fit your equipment's capacity. Every system has a function, and maintenance tasks can't be allowed to interfere unduly with that function. Tarsnap can conceivably saturate either disk I/O or the network, depending on your equipment, so you need the ability to limit the amount of bandwidth and disk activity Tarsnap consumes.

Limiting Network Traffic

If you have a fast disk and a lot of data to upload, Tarsnap can devour Internet bandwidth. While your network administrator can probably enable traffic shaping to control your bandwidth, you can also control bandwidth in the Tarsnap client. Generally speaking, it's best if the network administrator never develops a concern that you're backing up to an Internet service. They get downright cranky about utilization, saturation and stuff like that.[9]

The simplest type of restriction is to limit the total amount of bandwidth used to communicate with the Tarsnap service in a single session. The `--maxbw` option sets a maximum amount of upload and download bandwidth, which might be useful if you have metered bandwidth or a daily bandwidth allocation. You can specify a number of bytes, megabytes, or gigabytes. Here I limit a backup session to fifteen megabytes.

```
# tarsnap -cf docs --maxbw=15M docs/
```

Most people have unmetered bandwidth, but don't want a host to use so much bandwidth that it interferes with other hosts. The `--maxbw-rate` option lets you specify a number of bytes per second that Tarsnap may use.

```
# tarsnap -cf docs –maxbw-rate=125k docs/
```

Remember that Tarsnap uses bytes, not bits, and base 10 measurements. 125KB/second is one megabit a second.

When you run out of bandwidth, the client creates a checkpoint and exits. Further backups will take advantage of the uploaded, deduplicated blocks.

If you have asymmetrical bandwidth, you can set download and upload rates separately, with `--maxbw-rate-down` and `--maxbw-rate-up`. You can adjust your bandwidth settings to fit any environment.

Most people set these options in `tarsnap.conf`. If you've done so, but want to turn them off for a specific Tarsnap run, you can disable them at the command line. Each of these commands has a `--no` version, such as `--no-max-bw`, that overrides the configuration file.

---

9   Unless you're working with classified data, in which case "talking to the cranky network admin" beats the heck out of "going to the *special* jail."

Increasing Network Traffic

If your connectivity to the Tarsnap service is limited by network congestion, you can tell the client to create multiple TCP connections to the service with the `--aggressive-networking` option. This won't magically increase the amount of bandwidth you have available, but it might increase the percentage of that bandwidth Tarsnap uses.

For example, say Tarsnap is only using 1% of your company's overloaded Internet connection. Aggressive networking might let you crank that up to 3% or 5%. This steals bandwidth from other network applications, however. You get to fight that out with the other IT staff.

Aggressive networking won't help when the bandwidth simply isn't available. It also won't help if your network administrator has specifically limited Tarsnap traffic.

Limiting Disk Activity

You have a little more flexibility when it comes to limiting Tarsnap's disk access. Programs like nice(1) can de-prioritize the Tarsnap process so that it runs only when other processes aren't running. But Tarsnap also includes its own disk activity limiter in the `--disk-pause` option.

The `--disk-pause` option tells Tarsnap to stop accessing the disk for a number of milliseconds after it stores data on the service. It also pauses for that time after accessing every 64KB of data on the disk. Tarsnap reads 64KB of a file, and pauses. It reads another 64KB, and pauses again. It doesn't compete with other software at all during those pauses.

This option takes one argument, a number of milliseconds.

The exact effects of `--disk-pause` vary depending on the system and its load, but setting it to 10 roughly doubles the length of time needed to create an archive—or, if you prefer, it approximately halves the intensity of disk I/O during the backup.

If you've set `disk-pause` in the configuration file, you can disable it in a specific Tarsnap run with the command-line option `--no-disk-pause`.

Substitutions in Archive Paths

Tarsnap lets you change file and directory paths as you create or extract an archive. This lets you change where an archive will restore to.

Let's look at a realistic example, the `/etc` directory. I want to back up my system's `/etc`. Bad things happen and I want to be able to recover those files. I probably don't want to extract them directly into `/etc`, however. Even if I pull all of `/etc` out of backup, I probably want to restore only select files to the production `/etc` directory. Maybe my server was destroyed, and I'm restoring the archives on a new installation. While I probably want the password file and server configurations, I don't want to overwrite the new `/etc/fstab` or the new SSH host keys with the ones from the old server. And during a hurried emergency restore, when I'm under massive amounts of pressure, is *precisely* when I'm most likely to screw up. It's better to change the backup so I default to not overwriting the original files.

That's where Tarsnap's `-s` substitution option comes in. I can specify a basic regular expression using `sed`-like `/old/new/` syntax[10]. Here I create a new archive, but have Tarsnap look for the string *etc* in a file path and replace it on the fly with *oldetc*.

```
# tarsnap -s /etc/oldetc/ -cf etcbackup /etc
```

If I check the archive contents, the paths have changed.

---

10   "Let's say you have a problem, and you decide to solve it with Tarsnap's regular expressions support. You now have three problems."

```
# tarsnap -tf etcbackup
oldetc/
oldetc/profile
oldetc/autofs/
...
```

When I extract this backup, it automatically goes to the directory `oldetc`. I can safely extract this archive in my root directory and not overwrite the existing `/etc`.

You can use basic regular expression syntax with the substitution option. Symbols like ^ and $ work (although you must escape them as your shell requires). Similarly, for regular expressions that include slashes, you can use alternate separation characters. Here I tell my backup of `/etc` to always restore the archive into `/var/tarsnap/dr`, using a comma as a separation character.

```
# tarsnap -s ,etc,/var/tarsnap/dr, -cf etcbackup3 etc
```

I deliberately put the leading / in my replacement path, so that the restore automatically goes to this directory.

Again much like `sed`, you can put modifiers after the last separation character. Adding a *p* tells Tarsnap to print successful substitutions as it makes them. Adding an *s* means to perform the substitution on symbolic links as well as regular files. And a trailing *g* makes the substitution continue on after the first match.

Here I tell Tarsnap to print each substitution it makes.

```
# tarsnap -s /etc/oldetc/p -cf etcbackup /etc
```

Tarsnap supports other regular expression features, like capture groups and ~. A full discussion of regular expressions would fill this book, however. Check the Tarsnap man page and a primer on basic regular expressions for full details.

And any time you try using regular expressions in Tarsnap, I strongly encourage you to use `--dry-run` to test things first.

Archive Manipulation

You can use the double at sign (@@) to specify an existing archive as a source for Tarsnap archives. This lets you create trimmed versions of existing archives and rename archives.

Manipulating archives uses bandwidth and storage as Tarsnap shuffles metadata back and forth. Remember, an archive is a list of deduplicated blocks. Manipulating the archive means editing that list. No stored data blocks get moved between client and server, and the metadata required might cost you whole attodollars.

Renaming Archives

While you cannot directly rename a Tarsnap archive, you can copy it to a new archive and delete the old archive.

Earlier we created the archive *etctest-2014-12-23*. There's nothing wrong with the name of this archive, but after you create a few dozen archives it might easily get lost in the shuffle. Perhaps you've decided that all archives should begin with the name of the machine they're created on, and so you want to rename it. Give the new archive name with -f, and use @@ and the old archive name as the data source.

```
# tarsnap -cf mail-etctest-2014-12-23 @@etctest-2014-12-23
```

Now I search the list of archives for these.

```
# tarsnap --list-archives | grep 2014-12-23
mail-etctest-2014-12-23
etctest-2014-12-23
```

Both archives are there. If needed, verify the contents of the new archive with -t. I live dangerously, so instead I proceed directly to deleting the old archive.

```
# tarsnap -df etctest-2014-12-23
```

An identical archive still exists under a different name.

83

Trimming an Archive

Many of us create backups that contain vast swaths of data, but when restoration time comes we only want a small part of the data. One easy way to work on only the data set you want is to create a new archive that contains only specific files from an old archive.

For example, I archive the /var/www directory on my web server. It contains a dozen web sites. I suspect a problem in one site, and want to compare the site as it exists today with last month's backup. First, I check the files in the existing archive.

```
# tarsnap -tf www-2014-12-01-varwww | less
var/www/
var/www/black/
var/www/absf/
var/www/mwl/
...
```

My backup script (see Chapter 6) stores these files with paths from the root directory, but without the initial slash. I thought it did, but as I never remember, I always check first.

The files I want are all in /var/www/mwl. Here I take the archive *www-monthly-2014-12-01-varwww* and create a sub-archive of last month's archive, containing only the files in that path. Here I use the --include option to specify the files I want.

```
# tarsnap -cf mwl-only --include 'var/www/mwl' \
     @@www-2014-12-01-varwww
```

The archive mwl-only contains only the files that contain the string *var/www/mwl* at the front of their pathname. You could use other include statement options to make more specialized archives. If you wanted to create an archive that contained, say, the wp-config.php files from all your Wordpress sites, no matter what directory they were in, you could do something like this.

```
# tarsnap -cvf wp-config --include='*wp-config.php' \
    @@www-2014-12-01-varwww
```

I put a wildcard at the beginning of the file name because I want to include any directory path before it. I don't put a wildcard at the end because I specifically want to exclude files like *wp-config.php-busted-againyouidiot*.

If including files isn't a good way to create your sub-archive, exclude files instead.

Specifying Files in Files

Rather than backing up the whole system, you can create a list of files for Tarsnap to back up, exactly as with creating archives. Create a text file that contains one file per line, like so.

```
/etc/fstab
/etc/master.passwd
```

You can also tell Tarsnap to change its working directory by including the -C option in the file, followed by the target directory on the next line.

```
-C
/home/mwlucas
bin
.cshrc
```

This tells Tarsnap to back up the */home/mwlucas/bin* directory and all its contents, plus */home/mwlucas/.cshrc*. Because my shell resource file is incredible.[11]

End the file with a newline.

Tell Tarsnap to use the file list with -T.

```
# tarsnap -T /etc/tarsnapfiles -cf archive1
```

This archives only the files in */etc/tarsnapfiles*.

---

11   An incredible .cshrc? Yes. Incredibly crufty, with thirty years of detritus. I'd trim it, but it growls at me any time I approach.

Similarly, you can use -x to point to an exclusion file, precisely like when creating archives.

Miscellaneous Options

Tarsnap includes a few options that can be useful for particular environments and settings. Most of us will never need them.

To make Tarsnap prompt you for individual confirmation when adding each and every file to an archive, use the -w flag. This becomes annoying astonishingly quickly.

The --one-file-system option tells Tarsnap to not leave the current file system. If you want to create an archive that contains only the root partition, and back up /usr and /var and whatever other partitions you have separately, this is your friend.

The -n option tells Tarsnap to not recursively back up subdirectories in a directory. You'll get the top layer of what's in a directory, but nothing beneath it.

Tarsnap does not store file access time (atime). If you want to store atime, use the --store-atime option. Tarsnap must access a file to archive it, and accessing the file changes the atime. If you store atime, you'll archive an incremented atime on every file in Tarsnap every time you run Tarsnap. Storing atime increases the amount of bandwidth needed to use an archive. You can set atime in the configuration file to always store the access time. Use --no-store-atime on the command line to override the configuration file for a specific Tarsnap run.

The -c option changes Tarsnap's working directory.

Finally, Tarsnap automatically strips the leading slash from file paths when creating an archive. To keep that leading slash, and thus overwrite the existing system when you restore the backup, use the -P flag.

Chapter 04: Creating and Managing Archives

You can now make Tarsnap archives dance, sing, and play the Theremin for your amusement. Everything will be safely backed up. Now let's dive into some details on Tarsnap keys and the cache.

Chapter 05: Caches and Keys

Two often overlooked aspects of Tarsnap management are the cache directory and keys.

Tarsnap maintains deduplication information in a local cache directory. Most of the time you don't even think about the cache: it just works. Occasionally, though, the cache directory requires care and feeding. This is most frequently after a disaster, when you've lost all or part of your data, damaged your filesystem, or otherwise suffered an integrity failure.

Managing Tarsnap revolves around keys. Lose a key, lose access to the archives created with that key. You really, *really* must copy your keys to a safe place that's not on a server and not in Tarsnap. Tarsnap lets you do interesting things with your keys, however. You can encrypt the key with a passphrase, so that someone who breaks into your server can't access your archives easily. You can break up a key into several pieces, each with different privileges. Maybe your server can only create archives, but you delete archives on a different, more secure system.

While Tarsnap is designed to have one key per machine, if you're careful it's possible to share one key between machines. We'll touch on that briefly. But first, the cache.

Cache Basics

Each Tarsnap key needs its own cache directory. As each machine normally has one Tarsnap key, this usually translates to one cache directory per machine. Subkeys (see Key Basics later this chapter) are not truly separate keys, so they share the same cache as the main key.

If you have multiple Tarsnap keys on one machine, each key must have a separate cache file. You can use the `--cachedir` command-line option to specify the cache directory. Alternately, you could specify the cache directory in a `tarsnap.conf` file, and use the `--configfile` command-line option to point at the configuration file intended just for that key.

Tarsnap defaults to a cache directory of `/usr/local/tarsnap` because it doesn't need fast storage. If you've specifically bought an expensive high-performance disk for a special purpose, you've probably put it on `/var` or `/oracle` or someplace like that, not `/usr/local`. Don't waste expensive disk on the cache file, unless your whole system uses expensive disk.

Do not put the cache directory on ephemeral storage, such as a memory file system. A reboot erases these filesystems, so you'd have to rebuild the cache every time you want to do anything.

There's no good reason to back up the cache directory in Tarsnap. Or any other backup program.

Cache Directory Contents

The cache directory contains vital bookkeeping information Tarsnap needs to function. You must have a cache directory. Tarsnap's default cache directory is `/usr/local/tarsnap`. The cache directory takes up about 0.5% of the amount of data you store in the service.

The cache directory contains four files, all binary files not intended for human consumption.

The `/usr/local/tarsnap/directory` file contains and indexes the sizes and references counts of deduplicated blocks, as well as the cryptographic hashes of the unencrypted blocks.

The file `/usr/local/tarsnap/cache` contains information about files already deduplicated and uploaded to the Tarsnap service. If a file has not changed between Tarsnap runs, Tarsnap doesn't need to re-deduplicate or upload it. The cache file tracks file blocks and modification times so Tarsnap knows what it's already done. It might also contain the raw data from small files and perhaps even tidbits from the end of large files. Sometimes it's faster and more efficient to store really tiny files in the cache rather than run around collecting it all again.

Tarsnap maintains a lock with `/usr/local/tarsnap/lockf`. Remember, you can have only one archive creation or deletion process running at a time.

The `/usr/local/tarsnap/cseq` file tracks sequence numbers for Tarsnap deduplication. This file doesn't have any data in it, but is a symlink to the latest sequence number.

While you're not supposed to view or edit any of these files, if your cache directory is damaged you might need to manually remove one or more files so Tarsnap can rebuild it.

Cache Directory Security

Just how sensitive is this information?

If someone can read the cache directory, they can gather small parts of your data. If the intruder can tamper with the data and has enough Tarsnap knowledge, they could trick an archive delete command into deleting blocks required by other archives. If they're really, really good, they could trick the archive command into thinking certain blocks were already backed up, and thus not back them up at all.

The good news is, nothing in the cache directory is irreplaceable. If you've suffered an intrusion and you think your cache might be corrupt, destroy and recreate it.

If you use an encrypted filesystem, including the cache directory on the encrypted filesystem is probably a good idea. If you have an intrusion detection system like tripwire, or if you even regularly run mtree(1), you might check the permissions on the cache directory. An intruder who could subtly compromise your Tarsnap cache is probably capable of reconfiguring your local IDS, however.

Repairing Damaged Cache Directories

The cache is not invulnerable. You might lose the entire machine, including the cache. The machine might fail halfway through a backup. Two separate files might need repairs, the *cache* file and the *directory* file.

Broken Cache

If a machine dies at a specific moment at the end of a Tarsnap backup, you might corrupt the cache file `/usr/local/tarsnap/cache`. You'll know this when you get an error like this.

```
tarsnap: Error reading cache: /usr/local/tarsnap/cache
```

This isn't the whole Tarsnap cache directory; it's the file named `cache` inside the Tarsnap cache directory. It's corrupt. To repair the file, remove it. When you next create an archive, Tarsnap automatically recreates the cache file. The next archive operation uses extra disk I/O and CPU time, exactly as the first archive operation did, as Tarsnap caches information on those files. It won't use extra bandwidth or Tarsnap storage.

Broken Directory

The more complex situation is when you lose or corrupt the `directory` cache file. Rebuilding this file requires interacting with the Tarsnap server to gather the list of deduplicated blocks. Maybe you had file corruption due to a server crash or other system failure, or perhaps you used the wrong Tarsnap key with this cache directory. Additionally, you must rebuild the directory before restoring archives on new machine instances.

Tarsnap tells you if your directory needs rebuilding. Don't rebuild the cache directory on a whim, unless you like using extra bandwidth.

To rebuild the directory from scratch, use the `--fsck` option.

```
# tarsnap --fsck
Phase 1: Verifying metadata validity
Phase 2: Verifying metadata/metaindex consistency
Phase 3: Reading chunk list
Phase 4: Verifying archive completeness
  Archive 1/103...
...
```

Tarsnap scrutinizes every stored archive and copies its metadata back into the directory file. This might take a while, depending on how many archives the key has and how much data this key has stored in Tarsnap.

It's possible, but unlikely, that you have a corrupt archive. Corrupting an archive is really hard to do. The `--fsck-prune` option rebuilds the directory and removes corrupt archives.

You could also corrupt your cache directory by doing something clever and unsupported, like using the same Tarsnap key on multiple hosts. Let's talk about keys now.

Key Basics

I've said this before, but: back up your keys. If you lose a key, you lose all data stored with that key. Storing keys in Tarsnap archives is a terrible idea, because if you lose your servers, you lose all ability to access those archives. Back them up on reliable offline media. Print them in an OCR-friendly font and store them in a safe deposit box physically separate from your network. An average fireproof safe won't protect average documents during a house-destroying fire.

Tarsnap manages keys with the program tarsnap-keymgmt(1). This program lets you create new key files with limited permissions or create a new key file with a new passphrase. It doesn't alter the existing key file in any way, but only creates new key files as requested.

Whenever you work on a key file, I recommend making a backup of the existing key file and storing it somewhere safe. If you add a passphrase to a key file and immediately forget the passphrase,[12] or if you accidentally strip all permissions from a key file, you'll want be able to fall back to the original key file.

But let's start with key permissions.

Key Permissions and Subkeys

Tarsnap has four different privileges—list and extract, write, delete, and nuke. Tarsnap key files like we created in Chapter 3 contain four subkeys, each with one of these privileges assigned to it. You can pull these subkeys out of the main key file, creating key files with only certain subkeys and hence restricted permissions. The words "privilege" and "subkey" aren't exactly interchangeable, but they are tightly related.

---

12   If I can remember a passphrase 24 hours, I will remember it forever. But making it through that first day is pretty iffy.

Every time you create a new key file from a main key—either because you're assigning a passphrase or because you want a subkey file—you must specify the new key file's privileges. If you don't specify the privileges in a new key file, the new key file contains no subkeys and hence no privileges.

The *list and extract* privilege gives the key the ability to read existing archives. Specify this privilege with `-r`.

The *write* privilege lets this key create new archives. Specify write privileges with `-w`.

The *delete* privilege lets this key delete existing archives. Tarsnap cannot delete an archive without viewing it, so a key with delete privileges automatically has reading privileges. Assign delete privileges with `-d`.

Finally, the *nuke* privilege lets this key file destroy all archives created by the main key. It doesn't have any ability to enumerate the existing archives, it just burns them all down. Consider this a "delete" key without the implied "read" privileges—a pure "delete" key. Assign this privilege with `--nuke`.

Here I create a read-only key from my system's main key.

```
# tarsnap-keymgmt --outkeyfile readonly.key -r tarsnap.key
```

The file `readonly.key` is about half the size of the full key file.

You can create a key with multiple permissions. Unlike many other Tarsnap commands, you must specify each permission separately. You can't combine them into, say, `-rwd`. While `-d` implies `-r`, I prefer explicitly listing it on the command line because I'm insecure.

```
# tarsnap-keymgmt --outkeyfile readwrite.key -r -w -d tarsnap.key
```

This generates a read/write key identical to the original key. Why would you want such a thing? It's useful if you want to add a passphrase.

Using Limited Key Files

Let's try to use the read-only key to look at our archives. Specify the key file with `--keyfile`.

```
# tarsnap --list-archives --keyfile readonly.key
archive1
archive2
...
```

It works! Now create an archive with this key.

```
# tarsnap -cf test1 --keyfile readonly.key *
tarsnap: The write authorization key is required for -c
but is not available
```

The other key permissions generate similar informative errors when you try to use them for disallowed tasks.

Maintenance Privileges

Certain Tarsnap maintenance tasks require non-intuitive privileges. Table 1 shows various Tarsnap commands and the privileges needed to perform them.

Table 1: Tarsnap Privilege Requirements

command	privileges
--recover	either –d or –w or --nuke
--fsck	–w and –r, or –d
--fsck-prune	-d

Trying to run any of these commands without the necessary privilege generates an error.

Key Passphrases

Adding a passphrase to a Tarsnap key makes that key unusable unless a human being enters the secret passphrase on the command line. Passphrases are not suitable for automated backups, but can be good for Tarsnap operations you want only a human to do.

A good passphrase resembles a really long password. It should include spaces, words, special characters, numbers, and anything else you can type.[13] The passphrase is used to encrypt and decrypt the Tarsnap key. A key with a passphrase cannot be used until someone enters the correct passphrase.

Assign a passphrase to a new key file with the `--passphrased` option. Here I create two new key files from an original key, one without a passphrase for creating archives and one with all privileges and a passphrase.

```
# tarsnap-keymgmt --outkeyfile writeonly.key -w tarsnap.key
# tarsnap-keymgmt --outkeyfile rwd.key -r -w -d \
    --passphrased tarsnap.key
Please enter passphrase for keyfile encryption:
Please confirm passphrase for keyfile encryption:
```

The host using this key can now use the file *writeonly.key* to create new archives, probably in a scheduled automated manner. If someone breaks into your machine, they can run backups but can't delete any archives without your passphrase. You might even find the intruder's backups educational.

When you want to delete archives or recover files from the archives, you must use the read-write keyfile *rwd.key*.

```
# tarsnap --list-archives --keyfile rwd.key
Please enter passphrase for keyfile rwd.key:
```

You could perform deletions from a totally different machine if you desire. See "Sharing Keys Between Machines" later this chapter.

The key created when you register a machine has all privileges. To passphrase-protect that key, use the `--passphrased` option to `tarsnap-keygen`.

---

13   Your passphrase language choices are limited, as Unicode (sadly) does not support Enochian.

Sharing Keys Between Machines

Tarsnap is designed to use a single key on a single machine. It is *possible* to share a single key between multiple machines, but the practice is error-prone, strongly discouraged, and utterly unsupported. If you share a key and things go bad, you get to sort it out on your own. While copying the key file to another machine is perfectly easy, you must also synchronize the cache directories and carefully schedule Tarsnap processes.

The Tarsnap server lets each key perform only one archive creation or deletion at a time. If multiple archive-changing operations overlap, all but one fails.

The cache directory reflects the state of the archives on the Tarsnap service. It says what blocks have been uploaded and how many archives refer to them. Attempting to create or delete an archive with an incorrect cache directory generates an error. Tarsnap will demand you run `tarsnap --fsck` before performing any more operations. And creating or deleting an archive updates the cache directory.

Assume the servers Alice and Bob share a key. Alice runs its backup job and creates an archive. Before Bob can run its own backup job, it must get the current Tarsnap cache directory from Alice. This can be a pull (from Bob) or a push (from Alice). After Bob runs its backup, Alice must update its cache directory before it can run another backup.

This can go wrong in myriad ways. Especially on regular, automated backups.

You could run `tarsnap --fsck` before running each backup job, but this would take a lot of time and dramatically increase your bandwidth charges. Don't get me wrong, Tarsnap Backup Inc. will let you do this and happily take your money, but it's certainly inefficient.

If you're only intermittently sharing keys between machines, copying the cache back and forth between hosts with rsync might suffice. If your servers have a write-only key to run backups, and you perform archive management and deletion from a secure machine every so often, you might find the hassle worthwhile.

If at all possible, rather than use a single Tarsnap key on multiple machines, share the filesystems you want to back up with the Tarsnap host. Use NFS, SMB, or another file sharing protocol.

Backups are important, and Tarsnap is inexpensive. The gains of deduplication across multiple hosts are trivial next to the risks of broken backups or, worse, learning your archives are unrecoverable after a disaster. Use one or more keys on each machine.

The best way to run these vital backups is, of course, automatically. We'll talk about that next.

Chapter 06: Backup Rotation and Automation

The best backups are automated. With Tarsnap you don't even need to stir your carcass out of your chair to change the tapes every day. But you still must run the program every day, or every hour, or every week, to back up your critical files.

Tarsnap does not include an official backup automation and archive maintenance tool. The target users are Unix administrators from the whole spectrum of organizations. Some people use Tarsnap on a laptop, others run it on four hundred heavy-duty servers. Any single official backup script could not possibly be sufficiently flexible to meet every environment's needs.

Then there's archive rotation. When you're using tape backup, you reuse redundant tapes. People have invented all kinds of tape rotation schemes, such as grandfather/father/son, Tower of Hanoi, and "to blazes with it, just gimme that tape." You should rotate Tarsnap archives as well.

Let's discuss rotation first, then go on to automation scripts.

Tarsnap Archive Rotation

Tarsnap is cheap. Amazon has infinite storage space. Why wouldn't you just keep your old archives forever?

The more archives you have, the harder it will be to find the one you want. While one daily archive might not seem like much, in two years that's over 700 archives. I've had a server running for twelve years, spanning multiple operating system revisions and multiple server software versions. Imagine if you added a single piece of paper to your desk every day and never cleaned up. Shortly, you'd be buried.

Yes, you can list the archives in order with sort(1), but still, that's rather a pain. And most of those archives you'll never need. The only thing they can do is confuse you.

You pay daily fees for Tarsnap storage. Over time, they add up. Spend enough picodollars, and you start spending real dollars. One day, you will need to purge old archives, so why not implement proper rotation from the beginning and save yourself some pain later?

Start your Tarsnap backup regimen by including a process to remove unneeded archives. Implementing rotation at the beginning prevents annoyance later.

Backup Scripts

You always have the option of writing your own Tarsnap backup script. Many people have done exactly that. Before going down that road, look at the tools people have made available. The three I suggest here are Feather, tarsnapper, and ACTS. All three are used successfully by a variety of people.

Feather

Feather (https://github.com/danrue/feather) is built on Python and YAML. It's highly flexible, letting you run any number of backups at any time interval. Some files can be backed up every hour, others every month, as you like. This flexibility comes with higher complexity, however. If you need many different types of backup on one machine, definitely investigate Feather.

Tarsnapper

Tarsnapper (https://github.com/miracle2k/tarsnapper) is also built on Python, but implements the grandfather-father-son rotation scheme familiar to any tape monkey. It can also expire old archives created by other programs or by hand, giving you an easy migration path forward. It's less flexible than Feather, and less complicated.

ACTS

ACTS (https://github.com/alexjurkiewicz/acts), or Another Calendar-based Tarsnap Script, is written in pure `/bin/sh`, so it works everywhere. ACTS keeps thirty-one daily archives. 12 monthly archives, and never deletes yearly backups. This rotation scheme would waste many backup tapes, if Tarsnap needed backup tapes. It doesn't, so who cares? The configuration is a simple text file. ACTS also supports running a script before and after creating an archive.

I'm recommending ACTS for routine use, because routine tasks easily confuse a pressured, busy sysadmin. If ACTS doesn't meet your needs, then certainly check out tarsnapper or Feather, or look into the myriad other Tarsnap automation tools people have written.

Installing ACTS

Before installing ACTS, make sure you have a working Tarsnap install. Your host should be able to create and delete archives.

As ACTS fully automates archive management, it needs a Tarsnap key with read, write, and delete permissions. A write-only key won't work well with ACTS. Similarly, a passphrase-protected key won't work well—ACTS cannot enter a passphrase. (Yes, you could write a shell wrapper to feed the passphrase to Tarsnap, but if you're doing that, why passphrase-protect the key?) You can use ACTS on a key without nuke permissions.

Start by fetching ACTS from GitHub, either with Git or by going to the web site and grabbing the latest tarball. Pick a place to put ACTS. I normally put unpackaged scripts in `/usr/local/scripts`, simply to keep them out of directories managed by the package manager, so that's what I'm going to do here.

ACTS includes five files. `README.rst` contains basic information about using ACTS with Tarsnap. While I cover lots of that file's content in this chapter, always check `README.rst` for updates or changes.

The file `acts` is the actual ACTS script, while `acts.conf` is the configuration file. Copy `acts` to `/usr/local/scripts/acts`. Copy the configuration file to `/etc`. (You can put the configuration file elsewhere, but remember to update the ACTS script with the configuration file location.)

ACTS also includes two samples of scripts that can run before and after ACTS. These scripts let you do things like "create a database dump, then run ACTS, then remove the oldest database dump." They're only samples, so don't install them anywhere.

You're now ready to configure and use ACTS.

Configuring ACTS

Set how ACTS works and what it backs up in `/etc/acts.conf` and in `tarsnap.conf`. ACTS doesn't have many configuration file options, and most of the default settings work fine. If you set a variable to a value that includes spaces, enclose the value in quotes.

The only variable you absolutely must set is *backuptargets*.

backuptargets

Set the *backuptargets* variable to the list of directories you want to back up. List them relative to the root directory, excluding the leading slash. You must set this variable for ACTS to run.

```
backuptargets="var/www var/db/bk-mysql home usr/local/scripts"
```

I list here directories that contain server-specific data. I specifically include the `/usr/local/scripts` directory, so that ACTS captures my custom pre-backup and post-backup scripts. ACTS also uses these targets as part of each archive's name (see "Archive Names," below).

ACTS does not have an exclude syntax. See "Excluding Files from ACTS" later this chapter.

Remember that Tarsnap restores are slower than backing up. The easiest way to increase Tarsnap restore performance is to run multiple restores simultaneously. The easiest way to do this is to split your backups among multiple archives. Each ACTS backup target creates a separate archive. Creating a single archive for the whole system and excluding specific directories might seem simpler, but it really slows down restores. And aren't restores what any backup software is really about? Use multiple backup targets.

tarsnap

By default, ACTS runs `tarsnap` without any command-line arguments. If you want to add command-line arguments, set them in the *tarsnap* variable.

```
tarsnap="nice -n 20 tarsnap"
```

With this setting, Tarsnap runs at maximum niceness.

verbose

ACTS prints information about archive creation. If you run ACTS on a schedule, such as a cron job, it mails that message to the root user. Tell ACTS how much information you want in those messages with the *verbose* setting.

```
verbose=1
```

A 1 tells you which directories ACTS has backed up. When you first deploy ACTS, or when you change its configuration, use a verbosity of 1 to make sure it's working. If you get errors that don't make sense, try increasing the verbosity to 2 to get debugging information.

The default setting, 0, only produces output when ACTS has a problem. This is fine once you have ACTS in production, running on a schedule, and haven't changed anything. If your Tarsnap install is configured to print statistics, you'll get statistical output every time it runs.

A -1 tells ACTS to run silently. The only reason to always run silently is when you've already decided that you'll never investigate backup failures, in which case I must ask: why are you backing anything up?

hostname

ACTS uses the machine's hostname in the archive name. The default is to run `hostname -s` to get the machine's short hostname, but you can set this manually with the *hostname* variable or substitute your own command.

```
hostname=$(hostname -f)
```

Remember, all Tarsnap keys have a private archive namespace. You shouldn't need to change the hostname for Tarsnap reasons, but a different name might help you fit Tarsnap and ACTS into your automation system.

prebackupscript

Use the *prebackupscript* variable to run a script or program before archiving. ACTS starts archiving only after the script exits. I use a pre-backup script to do a database dump before archiving.

```
prebackupscript=/usr/local/scripts/mysqlbackup.sh
```

If the script never exits, the archive never runs. Also, the script must be executable.

We'll see examples of a pre-backup script in Chapter 10.

postbackupscript

Setting the *postbackupscript* variable lets you run a script or command after the archive completes. Here I use a script to clean old database dumps off my disk.

```
postbackupscript=/usr/local/scripts/cleanmysqlbackups.sh
```

Chapter 7 includes examples of a post-backup script.

The post-backup script must be executable.

lockfile

You can only have one ACTS session running at a time, mainly because you can have only one Tarsnap archive operation running at a time. ACTS uses a simple lockfile to detect running ACTS processes. The default is */var/run/acts*, but you can change the location if needed.

```
lockfile=/var/run/acts
```

If your server crashes during an ACTS run, you might need to manually remove this file.

Running and Scheduling ACTS

ACTS doesn't need any command-line arguments. Just run it. Here I run ACTS with verbose set to 1.

```
# acts
Creating yearly backup
Backing up etc...
Backing up root...
...
acts run took 55 seconds
```

If ACTS has a problem with one target, it archives everything else and then prints an error. Check your archive listing after the backup for error messages. Most ACTS error messages are self-explanatory:

```
Failed to back up "opt"! (tarsnap: opt: Cannot stat: No
such file or directory)
```

I listed *opt* as a backup target, but this system has no /opt. ACTS created all the other archives.

Once ACTS runs without an error, schedule it to run daily. To avoid flooding your network with a thundering herd of Tarsnap jobs, vary your backup schedules. Tarsnap runs on AWS, so it has copious but not infinite bandwidth. If many clients simultaneously create archives, they could slow down the service. The following crontab entry fires ACTS off at 1:45AM.[14] You can add something like this to /etc/crontab, /etc/cron.d, or whatever your system prefers.

```
45 1 * * * /usr/local/scripts/acts
```

If you have verbosity at 1 or more, you should get a nightly email. Don't decrease verbosity until you know ACTS works correctly when run under cron.

Excluding Files from ACTS

ACTS has no ability to exclude files from an archive. To exclude files, use exclude statements in tarsnap.conf.

As an example, my web server logs its activity in per-site directories under /var/log. I want to archive those directories, but not the system administration logs like the mail log, the messages log, and so on. I tell ACTS to create a single archive like this.

```
backuptargets="var/log"
```

---

14   I hereby call "dibs" on running Tarsnap at 1:45 AM EST. You lot, pick some other time!

Then I edit `tarsnap.conf` and exclude the logs I don't want archived. The operating system rotates these logs, so I must use wildcards to eliminate all variants on their names.

```
exclude var/log/auth*
exclude var/log/cron*
exclude var/log/debug*
...
```

ACTS will create a single archive for */var/log*, but that archive won't include these log files. This way, when I add a new web site to the server and create a directory for its logs, ACTS automatically adds that directory to Tarsnap.

Archive Names

ACTS combines the hostname, scheduled period, time/date information, and backup target in the archive name.

```
mail-yearly-2015-01-01_06:30:03-etc
```

This archive comes from the host mail. It's a yearly backup. It was created on 1 January 2015, at 06:30 and 3 seconds. (The time in the archive name is in UTC, not the server's local time zone.) It's a backup of */etc*.

If an archive is of a directory more than one level under root, ACTS removes the slashes from the directory. Here I back up */var/named/etc/namedb* on the same machine.

```
mail-monthly-2015-01-02_06:30:02-varnamedetcnamedb
```

This directory is the configuration information from a BIND chroot. I want to stash my DNSSEC keys and zone files in Tarsnap, but I don't need the rest of */var*.

ACTS looks for archive named with this pattern in its archive rotation process. If you use the same system for non-ACTS archives, ACTS will rotate them. Even if you really like this naming system, use something different for archives created by anything other than ACTS.

Small changes are sufficient—for example, when I create an archive by hand I use the ACTS format but use the word "manual" instead of "daily," "monthly," or "yearly."

ACTS Rotation

ACTS has a built-in calendar-based archive rotation schedule.

If no archive for the current year exists, ACTS creates a yearly backup. If no archive for the current month exists, ACTS creates a monthly backup. If both of these exist, ACTS creates a daily backup.

This means that the first time you run ACTS, you get a yearly backup. On the second run, you get a monthly backup. It can be weird to see a yearly backup dated 14 June, but that only means you started using ACTS on that date.

The archive created on 1 January will be a yearly. 2 January's archive will be a monthly. You get the first daily archive on 3 January.

ACTS keeps 12 monthly archives and 31 daily archives. It never deletes yearly archives. Once you decide that a set of yearly backups is obsolete, delete them by hand.

With the addition of automation, you now know how to create Tarsnap archives just about any way you like. Congrats, you're a Tarsnap guru—oh, wait. You probably want to know how to get your files back *out* of Tarsnap, don't you? Let's cover that next.

Chapter 07: Restoring Archives

If you're accustomed to working with tar(1) on tapes or files, recovering files from Tarsnap archives will be quite familiar. Tarsnap even shares some of tar's more annoying behaviors. We'll go through how Tarsnap restores work, then cover restoring individual files and whole archives. Many of the options usable while creating archives also work during restores, as we'll discuss.

Restoring Archives

Use Tarsnap's extract mode (-x) to pull files out of archives. Extract an entire archive by giving the archive name with -f. Here I restore all files in the archive *etcbackup*.

```
# tarsnap -xf etcbackup
```

The extract command runs silently, returning a command prompt when it finishes. If you want to watch it extract each file, add a -v for verbose mode.

```
# tarsnap -xvf etcbackup
x etc/
x etc/fstab
x etc/crypttab
...
```

If you want to extract a single file, give the full file path in the archive as an argument. If you're not sure of the file path in the archive, list the archive contents to find it. In this example, I'm looking for the

Plymouth configuration file. I know it's something like `plymouth.conf`, or `plymouth.d/config`, or maybe `etc/plymouth.d/plymouth.conf`.

```
# tarsnap -tf etcbackup | grep plymouth
etc/plymouth/
etc/selinux/targeted/modules/active/modules/plymouthd.pp
etc/plymouth/plymouthd.conf
```

The `plymouthd.conf` file looks right. Specify it by its full path in the archive.

```
# tarsnap -xvf etcbackup etc/plymouth/plymouthd.conf
x etc/plymouth/plymouthd.conf
```

This file is now recovered from the archive.

Next we have some ways to tweak Tarsnap archive extractions. This is not a complete list of extraction options, but rather those most commonly used.

Restores and the Extraction Directory

Tarsnap, exactly like tar, extracts archives in your current directory. And the archive creation process strips away the leading slash. This means that the location of your restored files depends on how the files were backed up and where you run Tarsnap's extract command.

For example, I back up my home directory on an OS X machine. The archive contains a whole bunch of files from `/Users/mwl`. The extract process recovers files using that same path. If I run the extract in my home directory, Tarsnap will create the directory `/Users/mwl/Users/mwl` and put the restored files in that directory.

To restore the files to their original location, either run the command in the root directory or use `-C` to change the extraction directory.

```
# tarsnap -xf homedirbackup -C /
```

Tarsnap will change its working directory to the filesystem root and extract the files

Not Overwriting Files

Depending on where you restore your archives, you might overwrite existing system files. Depending on what you're restoring, this might be really bad. A poorly thought out restore will damage your operating system installation.

Consider the example of restoring the backup of /etc. If I run this in my home directory, I'll create a /home/mwl/etc full of files. If I run this same command from the root directory (/), I will overwrite all of the files in /etc. How old is this archive? What has changed since this archive was created? Have I made configuration changes? I might even be restoring files from a destroyed system to a new system, in which case restoring the old files will disrupt the new system. The archive contains an incorrect file system table and incorrect SSH keys. Any hard-coded hardware-dependent values like MAC addresses or UUIDs or GUIDs are wrong, as well as a whole bunch of things I can't even recall right now. Dumping an archive of the old system's /etc straight over the live system will prompt a reinstall and a more thoughtful archive recovery.

One way to avoid overwriting existing files is to extract the archive in a different location. Specify an extraction directory with -c, exactly as in the previous section. Here I tell tarsnap to extract this archive in the directory /var/tmp.

```
# tarsnap -xvf etcbackup -C /var/tmp
```

Alternately, use -s to substitute a path on-the-fly, exactly as when creating archives. This example replaces the file path *etc* with *oldetc*.

```
# tarsnap -xf etcbackup -s /etc/oldetc/
```

Which method you choose doesn't matter, so long as you don't wreck your existing install.

Including and Excluding Files

The `--exclude` and `--include` options let you restore large chunks of an archive without reviving the whole thing. If you use `--exclude`, Tarsnap recovers the whole archive except for the section you specify. Here I restore my sample `/etc` backup, except for the `/etc/yum` directory.

```
# tarsnap -xvf etcbackup --exclude etc/yum
```

I could list multiple `--exclude` statements to not restore multiple files or directories. Here I restore nothing involving yum.

```
# tarsnap -xvf etcbackup --exclude etc/yum --exclude
etc/yum.conf --exclude etc/yum.repos.d
```

Wildcards are probably an easier way to accomplish this.

```
# tarsnap -xvf etcbackup --exclude 'etc/yum*'
```

I don't want the shell to interpret the wildcard, so I put the excluded string in single quotes.

Using the `--include` option switches Tarsnap so that it only extracts the files matching the desired pattern. Here I restore only the Yum files from this backup.

```
# tarsnap -xvf etcbackup --include 'etc/yum*'
```

You can combine includes and excludes with other options, like using `-s` and `-c` to avoid overwriting existing files.

Inclusion and Exclusion Files

Just as Tarsnap can read exclusion and inclusion patterns from a file when creating an archive, it can read these patterns from a file when extracting an archive. If you have a whole long list of specific files to include or exclude from an archive, include them in a text file, one file name per line.

A sample file based on my CentOS `/etc` archive might start something like this.

```
etc/passwd*
etc/group*
etc/hostname
...
```

Tell Tarsnap to include only these files with -T.

tarsnap -xf etcbackup -T etcrecover.txt

To invert it and have Tarsnap exclude the files listed in your text file, use *-x* instead.

tarsnap -xf etcbackup -X etcrecover.txt

Which should you use? Whatever makes your job easier.

Restoring Only Older Files

Some people want to use Tarsnap like rsync, only restoring changed files. Tarsnap isn't designed that way. The closest you can get is the --keep-newer-files option, which tells Tarsnap to not overwrite files that were modified after the file was archived. Tarsnap still downloads the complete contents of any extract files, but it won't copy the archives them to the filesystem if the existing file was modified.

Tarsnap Restore Performance

Tarsnap archive extractions run more slowly than archive creations. Reduplicating is more difficult than deduplication. With planning, you can vastly reduce the time needed to restore your archives. I *strongly* recommend restoring your archives to a test system so that you can work out any issues before you must do a real emergency restore!

Tarsnap uses the tar(1) format internally. Tarsnap stores its tar headers separately from the deduplicated data. If you're restoring a single file, Tarsnap must download the tar headers to find the blocks that make up that file. If you have several million files in an archive and want to extract only one file, Tarsnap must download the entire list of files in the archive. Extracting that one file goes quickly—once Tarsnap finds it! The extraction behaves much like extracting a single file from a large tar file or tape. This is a generic tar limitation, not a specifically Tarsnap-induced issue.

Tarsnap's restore speed is limited by latency with the Tarsnap service. If you have poor connectivity to the Tarsnap service, your file extractions will run slowly. For the best restore speed, have a fast, clean connection to the North American Amazon cloud.

The best way to accelerate large-scale Tarsnap restores is to run several restores on several different archives in parallel. The easiest way to do this is to create multiple archives per machine.

As an example, let's do a full machine backup and restoration.

Chapter 010: Full Backup and Restoration

Untested backups are not backups. They are, at best, a "Schrödinger's Hope" of restoring service after a complete system failure. Maybe your backup is good enough. Maybe it isn't. You can't know until you look in the box. Everyone who has ever been through a disaster recovery drill—or the real thing—knows that we back up in vague fear and restore in gut-stabbing panic. Always test your backups by doing a restore onto bare metal, either real or virtual. Yes, you must pay for bandwidth, but again, Tarsnap is cheap.[15]

In this chapter, we'll go through everything needed to back up and restore one standalone server. While automation systems like Ansible or Puppet can and should change how you restore and deploy new machines, this example gives everyone a common place to start from.

The Original System

This example web server runs a FAMP stack (FreeBSD, Apache, MySQL, and PHP) supporting several Wordpress sites as well as a few plain HTML ones. Tarsnap runs on schedule with ACTS. I want to slice this server's backups into several archives, so that I can restore them more quickly. I am deliberately not backing up operating system files or applications. If this machine dies, I will perform a new operating system install and reinstall all third-party packages.

A successful restore starts with carefully planning what you archive.

---

15   Multiple complete test restores of this web server, with multiple gigabytes of data, cost me less than $1 USD. Tarsnap expenses are *not* the limiting factor in tests! The true limiting factor turned out to be patience with my own incompetence.

Archive Targets

Figuring out what to archive is critical. Knowing your server's software and functions helps, but the only way to truly verify that you've backed up everything is successfully restoring service from the backup. That's why a restore test is so vital.

Most of the web site files, both Wordpress and plain HTML, are in `/var/www`. I have a couple special users with web sites in their home directories, and I'd like my personal directory backed up, so I archive `/home`. The `/usr/local/scripts` directory contains the server-specific scripts, including the ACTS pre- and post- scripts. The `/etc` directory contains user and system-specific configuration information that I shouldn't blindly overwrite, and `/usr/local/etc` contains package-specific software configurations.

Other archives are slightly more complicated. My web sites store their access logs in subdirectories of `/var/log`. I archive the web site logs, but not the system-specific logs. Chapter 6 covers this archive configuration.

The difficult archive is a backup of the MySQL server.

MySQL Archive

Databases use binary files as back ends. Don't back those up, with any backup software. Read the database documentation to see how to correctly back up the database data. MySQL recommends using `mysqldump` to create a database dump and back that up. Use ACTS' pre-backup and post-backup scripts to dump the database and clear old dumps.

For MySQL you'll need a user that can read everything in the database, but not alter anything. Here we create a MySQL user called *archive*, with the password *AwfulPassword*. You won't routinely type either the username or the password, so make them more complex than the example.

```
mysql> grant lock tables,select on *.* to
'archive'@'localhost' identified by 'AwfulPassword';
Query OK, 0 rows affected (0.00 sec)
mysql> flush privileges;
Query OK, 0 rows affected (0.00 sec)
```

Test your user to verify he can view everything in the database.

Now you need a script to create database dumps. This script creates a dump file, named with the current date, in /var/db/bk-mysql. Don't use this script blindly, but write something similar that fits your environment. You might prefer to put the password in a MySQL configuration file, depending on your particular prejudices.

```
#!/bin/sh
day="$(date +%Y-%m-%d)"
dumpfile=/var/db/bk-mysql/mysql-backup-$day
touch $dumpfile
chown 0:0 $dumpfile
chmod 600 $dumpfile
mysqldump -u archive -pAwfulPassword --all-databases > $dumpfile
```

Run the script to verify that it works, then list it in /etc/acts.conf as a pre-backup script.

```
prebackupscript=/usr/local/scripts/mysqldump.sh
```

ACTS runs the script and creates a fresh database dump before starting archive operations.

Automated database dumps are good, but will eventually fill up the partition. And they expand the size of your archive. Use another script to remove old dumps. This simple script removes everything older than 10 days. You can keep however many backups you like by changing the number of days in the script. They won't consume any additional Tarsnap space, but will take up disk space on the live system.

```
#!/bin/sh
find /var/db/bk-mysql/ -type f -mtime +10 -delete
```

List it as a post-backup script in */etc/acts.conf*.

```
postbackupscript=/usr/local/scripts/cleandumps.sh
```

Now add the dump directory */var/db/bk-mysql* as an ACTS target.

Final Preparations

Taking all of our backup requirements together, the original server winds up with this ACTS backup target list.

```
backuptargets="var/www var/db/bk-mysql etc home \
    usr/local/scripts var/log usr/local/etc"
```

Tell cron(8) to run ACTS.

Once we have a successful automatic archive, we can test the restore.

Restoring the System

The real test of a backup is: can it restore the system, or do you have to panic and scrabble? The real test of a sysadmin is: is that restore easy? Testing transforms an adrenaline-filled, nail-biting midnight death march into "run a couple commands and go out for gelato."

Test server restorations as realistically as possible. Pretend the original machine has been destroyed. If you find you need to copy something from the original server to the restored copy, the test has failed. Add that item to the archive and try again.

Script your Tarsnap restore process. People under pressure make mistakes. A sysadmin restoring a system from backup is either in her test lab, under a lot of pressure, or sufficiently burned out that she no longer cares. Writing down a restore procedure helps, but a restore procedure that reads only "copy this script, change the archive date, and go" helps more. You'll probably have to run your test multiple times to make the script work well, but repeating a test is better than repeating a real restore during a service outage!

A test recovery machine uses the same Tarsnap key as a machine in production. Do not create archives on the test machine. You can safely read another machine's archives using that machine's key, but if you create archives on your test machine you will create the cache synchronization issues discussed in Chapter 5.

Start by installing Tarsnap.

Install and Configure Tarsnap

Go back to Chapter 2. Grab a Tarsnap package for your operating system, or build it from source, or extract your existing Tarsnap tarball. Copy the host's Tarsnap key from your backup media, not the original server. Remember, a real restore test assumes that the original server has been destroyed.

With the Tarsnap key on the host, you should be able to list the archives from the original machine. Remember, archives (the lists of deduplicated blocks) are stored on the Tarsnap service.

```
# tarsnap --list-archives
```

If you can't list the archives, your key is corrupt. Check your key backup.

Identify Target Archives

The simplest way to identify the archives you want to restore is to look for the newest archives. Here I get the daily archives, view only the daily archives, and sort them in date order. Adding the `column(1)` command prints everything neatly.

```
# tarsnap --list-archives -v | grep daily | sort -nk2,3 | column -t
...
www-daily-2015-01-20_05:30:08-vardbbk-mysql    2015-01-20  00:31:06
www-daily-2015-01-20_05:30:08-varlog           2015-01-20  00:33:01
www-daily-2015-01-20_05:30:08-varwww           2015-01-20  00:30:47
```

The most recent archives have the date string 2015-01-20_05:30:08. All of the archives created in this ACTS run use that same date and time as part of their archive name, even though they were created at slightly different times.

With this information you can restore the archives.

Restoring Archives

While you can view a key's archives without a local cache, you cannot extract anything without a cache. Restore the local cache with a Tarsnap `fsck`.

```
# tarsnap --fsck
```

Tarsnap can now restore archives.

```
# tarsnap -xf www-daily-2015-01-20_05:30:08-varwww
```

Restoring archives is the slowest part of Tarsnap. Restoring a server one archive at a time takes quite a while. For fastest restoration of service, run multiple extract operations simultaneously. Here's where scripting comes in useful.

Below is a script I used to restore my web server's Tarsnap archives to my test machine. This script is deliberately simplistic, for illustration purposes, but perfectly usable as-is. You could give the archive date and time as an argument, or a shell variable, or any number of things. You could include triggers and handlers to announce when the restore finishes, or some `wait` calls, or any number of improvements. Once you know a basic restore works, add all the features you want.

Before running this particular script, I must identify the archives I want to restore. While the main part of the archive names don't change, I must update the date and time portions of each archive's name. A search-and-replace operation is much easier than remembering every step of the restore! (Pulling a setting out of the environment, or using a command-line argument, would be better still.)

```
#!/bin/sh

tarsnap --fsck
cd /
#These archives we extract directly.
tarsnap -xpvf www-daily-2015-01-20_05:30:08-varwww > \
        /tmp/varwww.log 2>&1   &
tarsnap -xpvf www-daily-2015-01-20_05:30:08-varlog > \
        /tmp/varlog.log 2>&1   &
tarsnap -xpvf www-daily-2015-01-20_05:30:08-vardbbk-mysql > \
        /tmp/vardbbk-mysql.log 2>&1   &
tarsnap -xpvf www-daily-2015-01-20_05:30:08-usrlocalscripts > \
         /tmp/scripts.log 2>&1   &
tarsnap -xpvf www-daily-2015-01-20_05:30:08-home > \
        /tmp/home.log 2>&1   &

#these we don't want to overwrite
tarsnap -xpvf www-daily-2015-01-20_05:30:08-usrlocaletc \
        -s /etc/oldetc/ > /tmp/usrlocaletc.log 2>&1   &
tarsnap -xpvf www-daily-2015-01-20_05:30:08-etc \
        -s /etc/oldetc/ > /tmp/etc.log 2>&1 &
```

This script runs every archive extraction almost simultaneously, in the background. Rather than print the output to the terminal, it logs the output of each to a file in /tmp. While this script exits quickly, the archive extractions continue running in the background until complete.

The script restores files like my web sites, old log files, and the like directly to their final place. It extracts the restored `/etc` and `/usr/local/etc` to different locations so I can more carefully merge their contents with the new system.

I have a copy of a similar script for each server in my small operation, stored on multiple web servers. Those of you with big server farms can probably use your automation systems to create restoration scripts at need, but test those scripts regularly.

Final Restoration Steps

This Tarsnap recovery won't get me a complete, working system. I chose to not back up my server software, like MySQL and Apache. They're easily installed from operating system packages. I must also merge critical server configuration files into `/etc` and `/usr/local/etc`.

Similarly, I must feed the latest MySQL dump to the database server.

You might do these installation and setup tasks with your provisioning system, or perhaps add them to your Tarsnap restore script. You can even do them by hand.[16]

Lessons Learned

What went well during your test restore? What was painfully slow? Change what you didn't like.

In my test, I found that my slowest restoration was the web server logs in `/var/log`. They're all in one massive archive. Splitting that archive into a per-site archive dramatically decreased restore time performance.

---

16   Maybe you can call manual configuration "artisanal server restoration" and charge extra for it.

The second slowest archive to restore was the database dumps in `/var/db/bk-mysql`. Each archive has eleven complete database dumps. Do I really need eleven of them? Probably not. My Tarsnap archives include the last thirty-one days of database dumps. A couple would be fine.

I also found that my backup didn't include a list of the software installed on the original machine. On the original machine I wrote a script to create a list in `/usr/local/etc/`, so I could easily reinstall those packages. Running the script daily keeps the list current.

Improve your archive regimen. Run another test. See how well it works.

Once you can easily restore your systems, you're better off than the vast majority of systems administrators. And with Tarsnap, you don't even need to leave your chair to put the tapes away.

Afterword

For me, Tarsnap is less about the cool crypto than about controlling access to my own data while still having easy access to recovery. The fact that it's cheap and that backups run quickly are bonuses.

With Tarsnap, intruders won't attack your backups to get your data. They'll go after your server instead. Or perhaps they'll go after you. Always remember that while the hypothetical "dedicated crypto-cracking hardware" would be quite pricey, "dedicated human-cracking hardware" can be purchased quite inexpensively at your neighborhood hardware store.

Ultimately, any backup system works as well as you make it work. But Tarsnap makes backups and restores so much easier than tape room spelunking. Although, admittedly, you will no longer need those sweet helmets with the built-in headlights.

Never miss a new release!

Sign up for Michael W Lucas' mailing list.

https://www.michaelwlucas.com/mailing-lists

blogs http://blather.michaelwlucas.com
Twitter: @mwlauthor

More Tech Books from Michael W Lucas

Absolute BSD
Absolute OpenBSD (1st and 2nd edition)
Cisco Routers for the Desperate (1st and 2nd edition)
PGP and GPG
Absolute FreeBSD
Network Flow Analysis

the IT Mastery Series

SSH Mastery
DNSSEC Mastery
Sudo Mastery
FreeBSD Mastery: Storage Essentials
Networking for Systems Administrators
Tarsnap Mastery
FreeBSD Mastery: ZFS (coming soon!)
FreeBSD Mastery: Specialty Filesystems (coming soon!)

131

Printed in Great Britain
by Amazon